Family Forever

John Thornton

Family Forever

For information about this title or to order other books and/or electronic media, contact the publisher:

Library of Congress Control Number: 2024900306

Publisher name: John Thornton

Publisher email: kbatto@ymail.com

ISBN: 979-8-218-96974-5

Cover and Interior Design: John Thornton

Technical Editor: Jamie Thornton

Contents

Dedication

This book is dedicated to my brother Joe and his wife Barbara. Their story is about total commitment to their family and friends. Doing whatever it takes to make things right against all odds.

The Events that occurred on the night of the hurricane and his very survival were only made possible by my Brother's lifelong dedication to defending his family. How many of us would have awoken and barehandedly attacked a person, pointing a gun directly at them? After reading this book, the reader should understand the meaning of total commitment other than to oneself by someone willing to sacrifice their own life if necessary to protect their family.

I am sure the reader will be surprised by many things in this book, but they are all true as detailed within.

Enjoy the journey covering over fifty years of a family's life.

Acknowledgement

This book would not have been possible if it weren't for my mother's influence. She taught me never to take myself too seriously and respect everyone who deserves it. Of course, identifying the people who deserve respect is a challenge, but I work through it when possible.

She informed me every day that something would happen, and she has always been right. When things went wrong, she readily identified it as "bad shit," and when something went well, that was just to be expected.

She possessed the gift of simplifying complex things by stating, "Always start at the beginning." And in tough times, you could still find something to laugh about even when things went wrong.

She has never heard many of the stories in this book, which, in retrospect, maybe a good thing.

I must also acknowledge my wife Kathleen and mother-in-law, who spent countless hours listening to these stories and encouraged me to write this book.

Enjoy!

Prologue

On August 29, 2023, the west coast of Florida stood and silently waited for Hurricane Idalia to make landfall. Idalia, billed as the once-in-a-century hurricane, continued to gain strength over the warm gulf waters. A once-in-a-century hurricane, maybe. It was a deadly destructive storm, without question. Above, a full moon hovered high, looking down on the dark, whirling clouds, and was the sole witness to what was occurring below. For those who live on the Gulf Coast, it is simply another subtle reminder of the downside of living in a tropical paradise.

The residents moved to and fro, covering windows, anchoring down furniture, gathering sandbags, and securing as much as possible of their belongings in what one could only describe as almost usual. As everyone sat and watched the minute-by-minute updates of the hurricane on the Weather Channel, it was more like a casino atmosphere in homes along the west coast of Florida. "I'll bet it tracks south toward Fort Myers," said Gary. "No, this storm will move north into the panhandle," echoed

Kathy. I shook my head; being a migrant from New York and never having lived through an actual hurricane, I placed my bet on the entire West Coast getting washed away and everyone with it. The only thing I was sure of was that first, I would be on high ground when the hurricane hit. Second, I would surround myself with solid block walls; third, I would have a roof over my head that could not blow off.

After all, hurricane Idalia was lurking a hundred miles off the Gulf Coast, and we felt ready. Or, I might say, "ready," as one could be staring down the barrel of a category four hurricane. Prepared for the storm of the century, yes. Ready for the events of the late evening of August 29, No.

Joe did not know for sure what woke him from his sleep. The squeak of the bedroom door hinges, the door handle's click as it turned to open the door, or maybe a flicker of light from the kitchen that should not have been there. Joe did not know for sure, but as he awoke, he made out the image of a man, a man standing at the bedroom door, a man, a man with a gun mumbling, "I'm going to kill you and your bitch wife right now. Cloudy-eyed and half-asleep, Joe jumped and lunged at the uninvited guest. Two shots were fired and absorbed by Joe's left shoulder in his effort to subdue the attacker. Joe instinctively wrapped his right arm around the man's neck, and they fell onto the bed where his wife was lying. The gun spoke again, blowing a hole through a closet door, and repeated the same short outburst, destroying a long mirror. As the struggle continued, Joe pushed his wife Barbara onto the floor using his right leg to put her out of the line of fire. Another loud burst from the gun punched a hole into a wall, followed by the weapon pressed against the right side of Joe's head, where the gun made its final report.

The assailant was now free from his grasp of Joe and moved out of the bedroom into the kitchen. The six-shot pistol was, for the moment, unusable, and the man searched his pockets for more bullets, the words used to make the gun speak, to reload again and finish his task. Unable to find the words in his pockets, the man gazed into the darkness of the kitchen, looking for something else, anything lethal, to finish the deed. The last thing the uninvited guest expected was to see the person he had just shot in the head grab a large knife from the kitchen counter and move toward him to attack.

The gun, worthless and now unable to speak, would be no match against the person the attacker believed he had just killed, standing defiant and wheeling a large knife. The uninvited guest fled through the unlocked garage door outside the home. Exiting the house, he jumped into the car he had left in the driveway and escaped. Joe stood, badly wounded, by the open door, holding the knife over his head, and waited. He waited for the attacker to return, probably with another fresh load of bullets to finish the job the attacker had started.

Joe's wait ended when he finally collapsed and drifted into unconsciousness, laying in a large pool of blood on the kitchen floor. The badly wounded body of Joe did not witness the screams of terror from his wife Barbara as she called 911. Joe did not notice his daughter wrapping his head in towels, trying to stop the bleeding. Joe was unaware of the EMT's arrival or transportation to the local trauma center. No, Joe was not aware of the dozens of officers starting the homicide investigation at his home. Joe was not aware that he may well be a victim of a murder! Joe lay unconscious, fighting for his very life after successfully defending his family from an attacker determined to kill both his wife, Barbara, and himself.

No one was aware of the fate of the uninvited guest less than five miles away and now cornered by the police. In his last act of desperation, once again, the gun, reloaded with the words found in the glove box, spoke. This time, the victim was the attacker himself, attempting to take his own life with a single shot to the head. The hand of the attacker finally released his anger, and his night of terror ended on a lonely street in New Port Richey, Florida. He died just as he had lived, alone and afraid, haunted by the demons from within.

Note from the Author

For a story to be considered complete, there must be a beginning, an end, and, unfortunately, a death. This story will meet all the criteria on a wild ride through life with many unexpected twists and turns.

Whether standing toe to toe with the 'bad guys' or confronting governmental authorities and the 'System ' when necessary, all with plenty of laughs and the craziness of family life along the way.

CHAPTER ONE

The Younger Years

Joe was born into what could be called a lower-middle-class family. He was the third of five children bearing the Thornton name, following his brothers John and Jimmy. After Joe came brother Richard and sister Debbie, the youngest of the Thornton family; this placed Joe right in the middle, exactly where Joe liked it. He was old enough to look over his two younger siblings and young enough to let his older two brothers take the heat when things went wrong. Maybe not always the perfect place to be, but that made little difference; we were a family.

Growing up in the nineteen-fifties and sixties had its challenges. Our father never had a driver's license, nor did he own a car. Everything the family needed would require walking, taking a bus to a store, or making it ourselves. Looking back, this formed the basis for our creative thinking, skills, and willingness to work against all odds. Our father worked as a cashier/cook at a local diner in Albany, New York, and collected 'bag money' dropped off at the restaurant from the mob's numbers racketeering. Okay, I know what you may be thinking, but a man needs to make a living, and in the 1950s, Albany gambling was an everyday thing, illegal or not. Whatever your feelings on how my father made a living, it does not take away from his ability to raise his family. He worked six days a week and earned enough money to support his wife and children. As I remember, he was never angry, but I also recall he never displayed fear. After serving on a warship in the Pacific during World War II and being at Pearl Harbor when attacked, fear would not be in the cards for him. The only time I saw tears in my father's eyes was when he talked about what happened at Pearl Harbor. Even tho I was very young, I could see the pain he felt deep in his soul about the events of that day. He felt pain, yes, fear, no.

Disaster struck when our father passed away suddenly from a major heart attack before any of the boys reached thirteen years old. As with most things in life, nothing is fair when it comes to someone dying suddenly, especially when that someone is your father. The person children must learn from and be disciplined by was gone, leaving four young boys to navigate the world alone.

Four young boys were now in the position of being an adult before becoming a teenager and trying to make correct decisions daily. I don't want to say life was all bad, but not all good. All the brothers were now a father figure, like it or not. When issues arose, the brothers would go to each other for assistance. We felt there was nothing we could not do and proved that every day. We learned right from wrong early in life and applied that to everything. The most important thing we learned was not to let others mess with the family. If you did that, all bets were off, and as my mother would say, 'bad shit' could happen and, in most cases, did happen at the hands of one of the brothers.

The plummeting economy of the seventies quickly followed the boom years of the nineteen-sixties. Cars were cheap, and gasoline was only thirty-six cents per gallon in nineteen-sixty-eight. Brother Joe was eighteen, six-foot-tall, with light brown hair, one hundred and six-ty-five pounds, and ready to take on the world. By all accounts, an average nineteen-year-old in the late sixties. As I remember looking back, we never really wanted or needed anything. Until his unexpected death, our father took care of basic needs. His four sons, my brothers, took care of all the rest. Were we wild? Well, no. Were we evil? No, not that either. We just became very protective of each other. We explored the city streets and places off the road. But wherever we went and whatever we did, we were together. We were just kids living and learning to care for ourselves and our families.

We got in trouble, had fun, laughed, and cried. Our father and mother both drummed in the reality of per-manently protecting the family; they are the only ones you can count on in times of need or trouble.

As for Joe, he was always looking for his next tempo-rary job to keep him afloat. Things were looking great for a young man starting during this period, and Joe was determined to make good on what appeared to be a never-ending boom for anyone willing to work hard.

Unfortunately, the sixties were followed by the seventies when reality began to set in. Even a person willing to work hard would need more than hard work to advance their future. The things taken for granted to be affordable by the "middle class" were drifting out of Joe's and everyone else's reach. Ever so slowly moving farther and farther away. Joe responded by becoming, as they say, "thrifty" in every way possible. For years, there has been a story going around the family about the first five dollars Joe earned, and he still has one. I can attest that this story is false as I have recently discovered he has all five of the first five dollars he ever earned.

Although Joe never took the time to finish high school, he was brilliant and quickly learned new things. Looking back, one would call it street-smart. He felt there was nothing he could not do, and he was never one to back away from a challenge. Of course, whether the challenge was dangerous depended totally on the outcome, either very good or bad. But, understandably, you think you will live forever or die trying when you're an eighteen-year-old male in the nineteen-sixties.

His social life was on and off, and Joe bounced around with different girlfriends and friends for the next few years. He developed a love for hunting, fishing, and golf and enjoyed an excellent bull-shit session from time to time, but always placed work first before all recreational activities. As far as drinking alcohol, Joe was at best a moderate consumer and left the getting drunk usually to others. He was always willing to help with a project and was unafraid to get his hands dirty. Looking back at Joe's younger years, Joe spent them developing the tools he needed for the rest of his life, and he put them to good use in raising a family.

One of Joe's many loves was the rifles and handguns collection. Joe kept his collection spotless and locked away in a small cabinet. He enjoyed taking them to a friend's farm and shooting them in the fields at different targets. When not target practicing, he hunted and always returned with a small buck or a story about the largest deer ever he almost "bagged." Based on the description of the size of the deer he almost "bagged," had he "bagged" it, the entire population of New York State would have had venison for years. According to Joe, the deer that got away was so big and tall that he would have only been able to shoot it in the foot. I went hunting with Joe occasionally and quickly realized hunting was different from my thing. First of all, it was done outside, usually in the later fall or early winter, which means it is cold, sometimes in the rain or snow. Imagine dressing up so something can't see you in camouflage clothing, possibly standing or sitting in the rain or snow, and hoping some idiot does not shoot you. Fun, my ass!

As I said, Joe loved guns of all types, and at one point, he acquired a Thompson machine gun. It was not precisely the weapon to go hunting with unless you planned to shoot down all the trees between you and your prey. But it was a great conversation piece, and when shooting a fifty-five-gallon drum, nothing in his small arsenal could compete. Like in the movie "Bonnie and Clyde," the machine gun ripped straight through a steel drum, leaving daylight shining through the holes. Yeah, it's probably unsuitable for hunting deer, but it has other uses.

Speaking of an unusual gun, a friend of Joe's in the Hell's Angels gave Joe a twelve-gauge shotgun for ten dollars. The "Angel" apparently needed the ten bucks for gas for his bike. Not that a twelve-gauge shotgun is unique, but one with a six-inch long barrel instead of the usual twenty inches made it much different. I think Joe called it "sawed-off." Yeah, that's what Joe called it, a sawed-off shotgun. I called the damn thing downright dangerous to hold, let alone fire! Of course, Joe took that as a challenge, and off to the rifle range we went, Joe, the little shotgun, and me.

After arriving at the rifle range, Joe took great pains to educate me about how to fire a gun of this type. Then he dropped the twelve-gauge shell into the chamber. He continued, "Hold the weapon firmly against your shoulder, lean forward, keeping your weight on your left side, pull back the hammer slowly, and squeeze the trigger gently. Don't pull it, squeeze it." The shotgun acted pretty much as I expected it to. There was a thunderous boom, a large puff of smoke, and Joe, who was once standing and giving me my education on the proper way to fire the shotgun, was now lying on his back, rolling from side to side in pain. Of course, I took the high ground, not wanting to insult my brother's expertise with weapons, and commented, "Nice shot, Joe." The fact that he was now lying on the ground, gun pointing straight in the air, moaning in pain, with his entire right shoulder black and blue, did not take away from the fine education I received that day on how to handle a shotgun correct-ly. The sawed-off shotgun proved dangerous whether in front of it or trying to hold it. I can note here right now that it was the last shot ever fired from that shotgun by Joe or anyone else. Joe was unaware of it, but on that day, I learned more about firing a sawed-off shotgun than he could have imagined. To sum up, Joe's gun course, Don't fire the damn thing, or bad shit could happen, which it did!

Chapter Two

Brothers

While Joe worked various jobs, I opened an automotive repair shop in Troy, New York. Thunder's Automotive was the sign painted on the building, and an auto repair business was born. The structure was an unused two-story warehouse large enough to work on ten cars. The converted warehouse was a perfect substitute for a repair shop. Two large overhead doors allowed easy entry, and ten-foot high ceilings gave plenty of clearance for small trucks. Should I have something to store? The second floor was empty for storage. Heating the garage in the winter was an issue, and searching abandoned buildings yielded a large furnace to do the job. As far as cooling in the summer months, sweat was the coolant, and it sucked. The only other issue was the location of the warehouse in what could be called a wrong section of Troy, New York. Luckily, I was young and too stupid to be afraid, and I adapted to the neighborhood. Besides, Joe gave me the sawed-off shotgun to hold for him, and I displayed it on the shop's rear wall. People entering the

8

shop could see the gun on the wall and figured I knew how to use it. No one knew I did not want to fire the gun as I had witnessed the result with Brother Joe, but on the other hand, who in their right mind would challenge a saw-off shotgun? Images of 'bad shit' were written all over it!

The garage was an excellent spot for friends to get together and hang out. It also gave Joe a quick place to go and fix his car when needed. As I remember, most of Joe's purchased vehicles needed full-time repair at my repair shop. I considered painting one of the stalls as 'reserved for Joe' on the floor so he would always have a place to work.

The winters in Upstate New York are long, and everyone needs something to do. Joe and I decided to purchase a used snowmobile to fill the long winter months with fun. Whenever I could take a break from working in the auto shop, Joe and I would take the snowmobile out and ride the many trails available or open to the public. When I said trails open to the public, I was referring to the local streets in Troy. Joe and I would take the snowmobile out and race the city streets whenever we had a good snowfall. After all, cars could not travel in the city streets' deep snow, so why not drive on them in a snowmobile? It makes perfect sense to two young brothers looking for something to do. The only issue was 'Is operating a snowmobile' on the city streets legal? Well, no. That is why Joe and I always wore helmets and masks, racing down the city streets looking for someone to chase us, as in the police!

In Troy, New York, there is a street named Middleburg Street. Middleburg Street is a steep hill starting at Oakwood Avenue and covers blocks as you descend. The ending street was Sixth Avenue, and the 7th, 8th, 9th, and 10th streets were between the Oakwood Avenue starting point and the bottom of the hill ending at Sixth Avenue. By any account, somewhere, you do not want to attempt to drive on during a snowstorm.

Our task was straightforward: find a police officer willing to chase people driving a snowmobile on the city streets, let him chase you in the police car, travel up Oakwood Avenue, and make a quick turn on Middleburg Street. Almost always, the officer would continue the chase down the steep hill, and I would pull over onto the sidewalk area and stop. Snowmobiles will stop on a snowy, steep hill, but a police car will not! Joe and I would sit there and watch the officer improve his driving in the snow skills as the car slid down the hill. An officer could not perfect these skills in a driving class; this was a driver's education at its best. We have yet to receive a public honorable mention for improving our public servant's skills, and of course, we never requested the honor either. After the training course, we returned to the repair shop and parked the snowmobile out of site in the back of the garage. Riding the snowmobile is how Joe and I spent our winter snow days, just having a good time with friends.

What made the snowmobile activities strange was that many of the Troy Police Officers were also my customers, and many times, the day after a 'training course,' an officer would come to the shop and check out the snowmobile they chased the day before. A big smile was followed with the officer saying, "We're going to get you guys next time." I would always ask if they knew when the next snow day was. With a handshake, the officer would leave, and all was well in Troy, New York, for two brothers just having fun, and frankly, I believe the officers were having fun, too.

Snowmobiles are great fun, but where do you keep that precious item during the warm summer months? Storing the snowmobile was the problem I faced, and it resulted in what could be called a final resolution to that problem. I decided to keep the snowmobile in my auto repair shop, the converted furniture warehouse, during the summer months.

The problem of storing the six-hundred-pound thing seemed accessible in a large repair shop. I put it in one of the shop's corners and let it sit until next winter when we could begin having fun in the snow again. Unfortunately, no matter where I put the thing, I constantly moved it to use the space it occupied. I quickly learned that snowmobiles slide much more easily over snow than cement floors. My daily exercise became transferring the snowmobile ten to twenty feet in the morning and then back again in the evening. As luck would have it, necessity is the mother of invention or at least the mother of an idea. The shop had an empty second floor with a wide stairway leading to the upstairs area.

It even had a large sliding door at the top of the stairs. All that was left was to devise a way to carry the six-hun-dred-pound snowmobile up the stairs where I would store it for the summer. Now, the only problem left to overcome was gravity. Once I beat that, the snowmobile would be in its home for the summer. My first thought was to ask my wife, Kathy, to help me drag the lead sled up the stairs. She declined with a quick "NO" before the final words left my mouth. I then considered rigging some hoisting equipment over the loading door on the second floor and lifting the monster, thus pulling it into the door. I quickly abandoned after considering the possible results of the six hundred pounds crashing to the ground.

I needed someone as crazy as me to help get the thing up the stairs. That someone showed up two days later in the form of my brother Joe. My brother Joe stopped in to check out a noise he had in his car's suspension. A deal was struck;. I would check out the car if he would help me move the snowmobile to the second floor. I drove the car into the shop, and it took no time to repair his vehicle as he tried to figure out the best way to get the snowmobile up the stairs to the second floor. He decided it was impossible to drag the snowmobile up the eighteen steps to the top, but if we could get the bottom of the snowmobile on the stairs, he could drive the snowmobile up the stairs. I stood back momentarily and questioned moving it up the stairs, but Joe quickly chirped, "I got this; watch and learn."

At this point, I was willing to try anything and gave the idea my blessings. Slowly, we worked the snowmobile's skis into position on the stairs, with the drive belt of the snowmobile pressing on the edge of each step.

Joe jumped on the six-hundred-pound monster, smiled, pulled the starter cord, and the engine roared to life. As Joe revved the engine, the belt began to spin at a high rate of speed, but the monster did not move. The drive belt could not get traction on the edge of the steps. What was needed was a little help, so I pushed the monster slightly forward with my right foot. As expected, that was all it took, and the beast, with my brother Joe in tow, climbed the stairs, possibly quicker than Joe hoped, at about 40 MPH.

It was impressive how quickly the snowmobile climbed the stairs at full throttle and how my brother Joe held on to the wild beast. The eighteen stairs were no match for the monster and proved Joe was right. The machine would have no problem climbing them. Everything was going fine until he reached the top of the stairway, where the monster and Joe crossed the ten-foot landing area and left the building through the second-floor door that remained open during the summer.

Like in the movies, the snowmobile and Joe sailed out the open door into the wild blue yonder to be met by his old friend, gravity. Gravity, being a sore loser, commanded that Joe and the monster come down, and down they came and landed in an empty parking lot across from the garage. Here is where the movie ended, as the landing was not as graceful as expected, and the monster shed a good deal of its weight, a thing called parts, and, of course, Joe.

Not seeming upset, I slowly walked to where Joe was now resting. I smiled and said, "Too much throttle," then turned and walked back into the shop, convinced the monster would be more accessible, stored by the open door until the junk man arrived to pick it up.

The following year, we did not purchase a replacement snowmobile. The images of Joe's flight out of the door were still vivid and haunted us for several years.

CHAPTER THREE

Joe Meets Barbara

After several years of bouncing between girlfriends, Joe met the girl who would become his future wife and life-long love. If I remember correctly, Joe and Barbara met at a party or gathering in Troy, New York, totally by accident. Barbara's sister Lori was supposed to be at the party looking for a date, and she brought Barbara along with her. A good rule is not to bring friends or sisters if you plan to hook up for a date. With Joe, on the other hand, it was love at first sight. Joe watched every move that Barbara made that night. I feared Barbara would move quickly, and my brother Joe would snap his neck, trying to follow her. As for Barbara, to this day, I am unsure of her attraction toward Joe. I felt confident that a young blond girl was not into fishing, hunting, and guns, and I knew Joe was not into social events. I do not know exactly why they hit it off, but from that day forward, all I heard from Joe concerned Barbara. On second thought, maybe Barbara was into fishing, and casting out her line, she hooked Joe. All I can say about the hook-up was that

Joe went from a proud shark prowling the open sea to a codfish on a hook. Joe became just bait overnight.

Barbara stood about five feet six inches in height. Not skinny like most young girls, but not fat or plump either. Looking back, it had to be her golden blonde hair and a big smile. That had to be it, as Joe did not have time to lay out his likes or dislikes at the party. As for Barbara, she did not say much. She just smiled and laughed when people spoke, funny or not. One thing I do remember is that Joe did not have a car at that time. I drove Barbara back to her parent's home. She did not say much on the drive home but smiled continuously. She did question me about Joe during the ride, and I filled in as much as possible where it benefited Joe. That was my job, the big brother laying out the welcome mat, telling her the good things about Brother Joe, and omitting whatever details might disrupt the flow of things. I made a point of not speaking about the shotgun incident at the rifle range and figured if he wanted to tell her about it, he would. I knew it would probably make her laugh, but I hoped it would not be a high point in Joe's prior life. Besides, if this relationship was going to start with a bang, I did not think the shotgun should be the thing making the noise.

Over time, I also learned Barbara had graduated from high school, and from what I could determine, she had a general diploma, not majoring in anything. She had a talent for drawing and painting at a level where her artwork looked almost real. And most importantly, the patience/personality of an angel would be helpful when dealing with Joe.

After that night, Joe changed. Nothing bad. Just different as things began to revolve more around Barbara. His normal activities took a backseat, and when Barbara was not around, Joe would hang patiently and wait for her, just like a puppy waiting for the owner to come home. I would not have been surprised if Joe started to bark when she arrived. I don't know what it was, but whatever it was, Barbara had it, and Joe had it bad for Barbara.

As expected, things moved forward, with Joe and Barbara almost inseparable. Where Barbara was is where you would find Joe. If I were looking for Joe, I would ask, "Where is Barbara?" and I knew that is where I would find Joe.

Things progressed quickly, and within a year, Joe and Barbara got married, and the once carefree brother of mine became the unthinkable "a married man." The birth of their first child, Joe Jr., in nineteen-seventy-two, followed. Things were changing; hunting, guns, and fishing were replaced by a full-time job and learning to raise a family. What the hell was he thinking? His ability to reason was quickly failing. I was unsure if this was the end of his extraordinary life or the beginning, but I knew it would be different. As it turned out, it was the beginning of a family, Joe's and Barbara's.

The most impressive part of this new family's creation was that Joe and Barbara still made time to support their original families. Night or day, a simple call would bring Joe and Barbara to assist in any project or problem that needed attention. Imagine something long lost today: a family doing whatever was required to support the combined family. I believe this instinct was born in each of the four brothers after the death of our father before we were teenagers. The need to care for each other was more substantial and robust every day.

Now a married man, Joe needed to work constantly to make a living. Joe's work history covered several jobs and skills over thirty years. One of Joe's first jobs was with Barbara's father's carpet installation business. Joe was a carpet installer working for Barbara's father for several years. Joe learned the trade very quickly and found installing carpets somewhat fulfilling. A job Joe could do and step back to admire the improvement his efforts had made to someone's home. It also meant Joe could take the extra carpet scraps and use them elsewhere. I cannot count the times I saw Joe sew a pile of scrap pieces together and carpet an entire room for another family member. When Joe had completed putting the pieces together, it was impossible to tell if it was not a single piece of carpet. Joe was carpeting his family's homes using leftovers and scrap carpets, and no one could tell it was not a new carpet.

This early job allowed Joe's family to live in a modest rented flat in Troy, New York, on a less than-convenient third floor on 5th Avenue. It was not perfect, but it was what the family could afford on Joe's pay. Joe also knew this job would be a stepping stone to a better job. While living on 5th Avenue in Troy, Spring Bobby Jo, the second child of Joe and Barbara, was born.

When Barbara's father closed the carpet company, Joe needed a new job. Joe followed the carpet installation job by working in an automotive machine shop in Troy, New York, for about three years. Joe further developed his skills in repairing and maintaining cars and other machines. This three-year hands-on education would be vital for Joe to create the things his family would need in the coming years. After leaving the machine shop, Joe followed up with a position with Hess Oil Corporation, and Joe remained there for over twenty years.

Along with this new job, Joe moved his family from the 5th Avenue apartment in Troy to a more convenient location for work. It took almost nine years for Joe to get to this point. Nine years of hard work at varying jobs. Finally, he was a manager for Hess Oil and felt confident his family could afford to move to a place closer to where he worked.

This move landed the family in The Phalen Court Apartment complex for low-income families. It was closer to his work and allowed him to save money to purchase his dream farm. At the Margaret W. Phalen Apartment complex, Joe and his family discovered the true evils of people. It happened in the summer of nineteen-seventy-nine.

The Margaret W. Phelan Apartments is a complex consisting of eighty-nine townhome-style apartments, a community center, and a maintenance garage. The complex has ten four-bedrooms, twenty-six three-bedrooms, and thirty-six one-bedroom. The site is several hilly blocks from a major Capital District Transportation Authority bus route, and it is located on a picturesque hill just a few blocks from a large City of Troy recreation facility. The bottom line is that the facility is a low income project and comes with all the problems found nation-wide in this type of housing. Nowhere to be found in this description is the fact that your chance of being assaulted is very significant, robbery could be a daily occurrence, and fighting with the neighbors is considered normal!

On my first trip to my brother's house in Phelan Apart-ments, I would describe it as, after ascending the several hilly pothole-laden blocks leading to the picturesque hill overlooking what remains of the built-in eighteen hun-dred decayed homes in South Troy, New York, you arrive at the Margaret W. Phelan Apartments. The streets in the complex are all single-lane, one-way, thru fares with the 'townhome-style apartments located on both sides of the street. The lower part of each 'townhome-style' home is brick, with gray siding covering the upper portion. You will also find the streets narrow and winding between the rows of apartments, limiting your view of approaching hazards. Welcome to Phelan Court Apartments in Troy, New York, in nineteen-seventy-nine.

CHAPTER FOUR

The Good Neighbors

J oe arrived home from work shortly after five that afternoon. His new job as a Hess gas station manager was a big move in his career, and he felt good about himself. Sliding out of his newly purchased car was a pleasant relief from the previous junk cars he was used to driving. Finally, all of his hard work was beginning to pay off. Now he could afford a new car, not an expensive one, but a new one.

The warm air hit him right in the face as he exited the car. It is another warm summer day in Upstate New York, with temperatures reaching the upper eighties. Joe had parked his car outside in front of his apartment, climbed the two steps of the front porch, and went inside. He found Barbara working in the kitchen and the young kids playing in the living room.

He took off the heavy steel-toed work shoes he had dragged around all day and sat down for the first time in what seemed to be hours. Finally, he sat back, if only briefly, but tonight, there would be no rest; the craziness was about to begin. It was Joe Jr. who sounded the alarm, "Daddy, there's a kid outside dumping dirt on the car!" "What," Joe responded, getting up from the soft chair to look. Gazing out the front window, he saw a small boy, about four or five, dumping dirt from a small pail onto the front of his new car. He exited the front door and barefoot walked over to where the car lay at rest. "Please, son," Joe said in a friendly voice, "don't do that, okay?" Almost as if he was asking the little boy a question.

The unbelievable happened as the little boy turned and began to walk away. Sitting on an adjacent porch, the little boy's mother screamed, "He can dump dirt on that car! You have no right to have a new car and live in this project," followed without a breath. She commanded her son to refill the pail and dump it on the car again. Joe, still barefoot, positioned himself between the small boy and the car. "Please, we don't want any trouble. My family and I want to live here and not have any problems with anybody, please," Joe pleaded. The woman did not want to hear any of the pleadings and again directed the boy to refill the pail with dirt and dump it on the car.

Joe positioned himself directly between the boy's path and the car. He stood quietly, waiting for the woman to recall her son and end the issue. Instead of disciplining her son, the woman called down the street to her boyfriend and two men standing with him. The three men moved slowly but steadily up the street to where the woman was seated. Her boyfriend's loud mouth shouted, "What's wrong now bitch!" The woman pointed to Joe and laid out her version of a right for her son to dump dirt on anything he wanted to, new or not. Joe just stood there silently and watched the men weigh their next move.

The three men slowly moved towards Joe, and as they did, they separated enough to make Joe feel surrounded or trapped. Joe still did not move. The loudmouth boyfriend spoke first, "Are you giving my girlfriend a problem, buddy?" Joe calmly spoke. "All I want is for the little boy not to dump dirt on my car. Look, my family and I don't want any trouble, so let's forget about this, and it is over, okay," As Joe waited for an answer, he could sense the three men standing there believed, incorrectly, they had spotted weakness or fear. Joe never blinked, even with three men standing toe to toe with him. From the corner of his eye, Joe could now see Barbara standing on his front porch, waving for Joe to return inside the house. The loud boyfriend was not going to let an opportunity like this slip out of his hands, and again in a loud voice, "And when we are done with you asshole, I am going to go up there and slap that stupid bitch of yours." He followed that up with, "And screw your kids too!"

Mistakes can be made, and mistakes will happen, and Mr. Loudmouth made a bad one. He threatened Joe's family.

Standing there barefoot, Joe was significantly disadvantaged against the three men. Joe stood momentarily and summed up the three standing before him. Joe glanced at each of the men's pockets for the bulge of a weapon, but he was still unsure if they had something to fight with, and he had no shoes on his feet, which was not the position he wanted to be in. He remembered our mother saying always start at the beginning, and the beginning meant putting on shoes for the possible upcoming fight. Our mother also told us not to turn our back on trouble, and Joe felt this might qualify as trouble to Mom.

Joe slowly moved onto his front porch with the three men closely following him. Entering the house, he quickly slipped on his steel-toed shoes and again emerged. Pausing briefly at the top of the stairs, Joe evaluated the three men. Okay, he said to himself. The loudmouth boyfriend is the 'ringleader,' him first. The guy on the left is the bigger of the remaining two, him second. And then the more petite skinny guy last. The boyfriend did not know it, but his loud mouth had made a grave mistake; he threatened Joe's family!

Joe carefully stepped off the porch, and the three men moved slightly back to make room for the beating they would give Joe. As soon as Joe's feet became planted solidly on the cement, his right foot, with the heavy steel toes, contacted the loud boyfriend's nuts. The boyfriend went straight to the ground, screaming as he went. In the same move that took down the boyfriend, Joe ducked and came up behind the larger of the two other men. Unfortunately for this man, Joe had him in a 'headlock' choking the wind out of him. This man dropped within seconds without the benefit of air, and Joe quickly turned to the third skinny guy. From all accounts, the third man ran down the street and would have set an Olympic record as he went.

During all of this, Barbara did not even have time to scream. Joe slowly moved back up onto his porch while the two men attempted to drag their asses back toward the girlfriend's porch. Still, the peace was not to be had tonight, even with the main event over. Barbara grabbed Joe's arm and directed him to look up the street, where a gang of men approached quickly, wheeling baseball bats, pipes, and anything else they could hold. They were coming and, without question, going to destroy anything and injure anyone associated with Joe. As Barbara stood briefly on the porch, Joe entered the house. Opening the closet, Joe grabbed the equalizer, the 30 ought six hunting rifle, and pushed the clip containing the shells into the rifle's slide. Joe's exit from the house onto the front porch carrying the rifle was as dramatic as anything in the movies. The crowd stopped about forty feet from the porch and remained silent. Not a single person, not one, in the group raised their hand and yelled, "Let's get him."

In a panic, Barbara ran into the house and called the police for assistance. The call brought the police with many cars blocking off the street from several directions. As the police arrived, the baseball bats, pipes, and other weapons disappeared under parked cars. It was at this point that the people in the crowd began telling the police that Joe had threatened them with a gun for some unknown reason. The police arrested Joe for having a loaded firearm within city limits and then arrested Barbara when she protested Joe's arrest. The loudmouth boyfriend claimed Joe assaulted him again for some unknown reason. After that, Joe and Barbara were loaded into police cars while the group cheered. Joe and Barbara were taken to Jail to be held by the police for assault with a deadly weapon. Joe's two young children were left unattended in the apartment by the police, with an angry crowd hanging outside. Alone in the apartment, the two children huddled for safety and waited for someone to come and help.

The call came about six-thirty from Joe at the Jail to his brother John. Joe gave John a brief description of what happened, but most important was the information about the children being left alone at the house. John left immediately and picked up his brother Richard on the way. They went to the apartment to recover the children left alone and pick up the car before the friendly neighbors destroyed it. While at the apartment, a group of friendly neighbors gathered around chanting, "We are going to get you, we are going to get you," as they moved back and forth along the street. Richard and I looked at each other as we watched these idiots. They did not know Brother Joe was the friendliest of the four brothers, but the night was early, and first, we needed to get the children out of harm's way.

The apartment, now secured, and the children and car moved to John's home for safekeeping, gave us the needed time to form our plan. That extra time is what we needed for Brother Richard and me to decide what we would do next and how to handle the friendly neighbors at the apartment complex.

We had a lot of loose ends to deal with. Joe and Barbara were in Jail, and the apartment containing all their possessions was left unprotected. And there was little doubt in our minds the apartment would be broken into during the night and everything taken or destroyed. Richard and John broke the tasks into pieces and decided that Brother Richard would rent a truck and enlist Tommy to help move their possessions. I would bail out Joe and Barbara and then meet Richard and Tommy back at my house, giving us time to go to the apartment during the last daylight and get the house emptied before the wonderful neighbors could trash the place.

The friendly neighbors already had a "run-in" with brother Joe, and soon, it would be time to meet brother Richard and John from the family along with a good friend, Tommy. I headed to the police station to bail out Joe and Barbara while Richard picked up Tommy and got the truck. A car drove up as I waited outside the station for the booking paperwork charging Joe and Barbara. Two men and a woman climbed out of the back seat and, as best I can describe, a beat-up car. One man moved erratically as he walked as if riding a horse too long. He looked as if he were in bad pain. As I stood to one side, he pointed at me and said, "Isn't that his brother?" He moved as if he were going to come over to where I was standing when the second man grabbed him by the arm. "The brother that did this to us is the nicer of the two, and I'd leave that one alone. He is the one Big Charlie from the pool hall called Thunder. Please stay away from him; he is bad news!" With that, they moved along and into the station to file their assault complaint against Brother Joe.

Five hundred dollars to bail Joe and Barbara out. Five hundred dollars! I laid out the bail money to the officer at the desk, and another officer went down to the cells and got Joe and Barbara. With that paid, I transported Joe and Barbara to my home, where I met with Richard and Tommy. From there, it was back to load a truck and meet the friendly neighbors.

The trip was only about six miles, but traveling in Troy, New York seems like a hundred miles with all the narrow one-way streets and potholes. The low-income housing Joe and Barbara lived in was on top of a hill with winding pot-holed roads leading into the main street. I would want to live somewhere else. But Joe had it all figured out: rent there until he could save a little money and maybe get a farm. I am glad he did not "buy the farm" while they lived there, if you know what I mean.

Richard slowly moved the truck in line with Joe's apartment and sat there momentarily, looking at the crowd of good neighbors that had gathered. "What are you looking at?" was my question to Richard as he delayed backing up the truck. "I am looking for the big 'L,'" he replied. I responded, "What big 'L' are you talking about." Richard gave me a slow head turn and replied, "The big 'L' on the foreheads of these losers, that big 'L,'" then he paused. At that point, Richard carefully backed the truck up to the two-step porch in front of the apartment.

The height of the porch made loading the furniture very easy; household items could be carried up the ramp directly into the truck. Once parked, Richard, Tommy, and I entered the beautiful world of crazy people in a low-income project. What they say is true: if you have nothing, there is nothing to lose! Looking around at the crowd, I realized these people had nothing to lose. I then thought to myself, if needed, I would give them something to lose.

We moved the larger pieces of furniture into the front of the truck, leaving smaller items at the rear in case Joe or Barbara needed something. Night fell, and we were still moving the last of the more minor things from the closets. I searched a bedroom closet and removed Joe's hunting and fishing equipment. On the top shelf, I found a large hunting knife in its sheath, with a fish scaler along the back edge and very sharp. To be sure no one would get hurt with it, I slid the sheath containing the knife down the back of my pants, secured by my belt. Now, I felt that a dangerous knife like that would hurt no one, well, maybe. As we continued, Richard worried that someone might let the air out of the truck's front tires, and we would not be able to leave. Being stranded at night with a growing crowd of less-than-friendly neighbors would not be a good idea. I walked around the truck to make Brother Rich feel better, checking for problems. As I turned the passenger side corner of the truck, a tall man stepped into my path. "What makes you think we're going to let you leave with that stuff," he said as he glanced back at the crowd and displayed his bravery. I was hoping these people would just let us leave, but that was not the case, at least as far as they were concerned. Before he could finish his sentence, I drew the hunting knife that had inadvertently slid into my belt. As the knife was pressed up against his throat and held solidly, I commented, "I'm betting your life on it!"

The crowd began to back away from what was happening between the man and me. "If anyone comes near this truck, I am coming back and cutting their eyes out," echoed from deep within me. The man with the knife at his throat had tears in his eyes as any quick movement might be his last. The man fell to the ground and crawled away from the truck. I stepped toward the crowd, and they stepped back. Making sure the crowd understood what I meant, I repeated my warning, "Any problems here, and I will come back and finish this. Do you understand me, and do I need to come over there and show you, good people, what I mean?" No one moved forward to confront me, no one. I think the group realized they did have something to lose after all, and keeping us from leaving with the truck was not worth the loss.

When I returned to loading the truck, Richard asked, "What took you so long to check the tires?" I replied, "I needed to speak with someone at the front of the truck, that's all." The loading of the last of the items took about twenty minutes to complete, and with the truck now loaded, we closed the doors and slid the loading ramp back into the truck.

Before we climbed into the truck to leave, we could see the crowd was noticeably fewer. Richard looked at me as we stood on the sidewalk before saying, "Looks like whatever you told them, they understood." With Richard at the truck's wheel, we took our last look at the good neighbors and the project. We drove away back down the pothole-filled roads, leaving the paradise the friendly neighbors had created. I remember thinking Barbara and the children were safe from the friendly neighbors. Then, of course, with Joe not being there to move his property with us, the neighbors would also be safe from Joe's grips.

Phelan Court Apartments

CHAPTER FIVE

The Plea Deal

Joe and Barbara were facing charges with several felony counts ranging from brandishing a loaded weapon within city limits, assault with a deadly weapon, causing a riot, physical assault, and a few misdemeanors to balance things out. Not a single word about what happened that night. The good neighbors had won a battle, but Joe was getting ready to win the war. The war was about to begin at his public defender's office a few weeks after the event. Their appointment was on a Tuesday in the early afternoon in Troy, New York, and Joe and Barbara would not be late.

The door to the small office opened with a slight creaking sound, bringing into view the walls lined with books. Law books were everywhere, on almost every wall. Joe poked at Barbara. We're not smart enough to read what is in these books, but I know what they say. "The party of the first part gets to screw the party of the second part, which leads to the lawyers getting all the money from both parties – plus interest," this was Joe's rendition of the legal terms of what the books contained. Barbara poked back and smiled, "I don't believe that – that's not really in them – is it?" As she remarked with a straight face, Joe was unsure whether to believe her. Before they could take a second step into the office, a voice behind a small desk said, "I believe you are the Thorntons. Please sit, and your attorney will be with you shortly."

Joe was still determining who the court-assigned attorney was, but after evaluating the office, he felt sure it was not Perry Mason. After a short wait, another door opened, followed by a deep voice, "Come on in, folks – I'm Jerry Flink, your appointed attorney." Joe and Barbara glanced at each other, stood up, and moved into the next office. The lawyer was again seated behind his desk and wasted no time summarizing the case against Joe. Let's see here, said Mr. Flink. "You are charged with possession of a loaded weapon within city limits, assault with a deadly weapon, inciting a riot, battery, and some other minor misdemeanors." He continued without even looking up. "I have already spoken with the prosecutor and the Judge. We have agreed to six months in jail, a one-thousand-dollar fine, and loss of your privilege to own a firearm. Now, of course, you will need to pay for the injuries to your male victim, but it should not be more than around ten thousand dollars. Now, how is that for a great deal, Mr. Thornton?"

Joe sat back in his chair momentarily and said, "And what happened to the woman and the guys who caused all this to go down?" Flink, looking bewildered at Joe's comment. Flink replies, "Well, they are the victims, and nothing happens to them." Joe's face tightened up, "Victims – victims, are you kidding – they were going to beat me, they were going to wreck my car, they threatened my family, and they are the victims? I, no, we, are the victims here, not them. They are a bunch of lowlifes, sitting on public assistance waiting to see what trouble they can cause. I am not pleading guilty to anything, and you let the prosecutor know! I want a trial, and I will show everyone how corrupt this system is; I want a trial!"

The meeting with the attorney ended quickly, and Joe and Barbara left the office of their savior/attorney, refusing to make a deal to close this ridiculous case by the prosecutor. Joe decided to return to work, and Barbara returned to my house to search for a new place to live.

The answer from the prosecutor came the next day in a letter to Joe's attorney. The letter read in part, "We are going to pursue these charges and enforce them to the full extent of the law. The evidence is overwhelming, and a jury will convict Mr. Thornton, who will be facing fifteen years in state prison for these crimes. Please inform your client about the gravity of this case and the likely outcome of a lengthy prison sentence." Attorney Flink reads the letter slowly to Joe over the telephone, giving it time to sink in. When the attorney finished reading the letter, he waited for an answer from Joe. Joe answered quickly: "We're going to trial, and you let them know I plan to expose these idiots for who they are. We are going to trial, do you hear me? We are going to trial! The prosecutors we hire to protect us, and instead, they defend the criminals. They are idiots, do you hear me?

They are idiots!" With that said Joe hung up the telephone and returned to work.

The court dates were set and canceled several times over the next six months. Something always came up where the case could not move forward. Delay after delay led to six months of waiting for his day in court. Unable to move forward with his life, Joe demanded a meeting with his attorney, the Judge, and the prosecutor. With all present in the Judge's Chambers, the prosecutors presented their side of the case to the Judge. The Judge sat back and requested the information on any plea offered before continuing. The prosecutor detailed the sweet deal of six months in jail, a fine, and loss of gun privileges. The Judge smiled, "Well, that seems like a very fair deal to me. How about it, Mr. Thornton?" "No, No, Hell No!" was Joe's response as he stood up from his chair. "They threatened my family, and they should be going to trial, not me; you are all idiots." Joe finished for the moment. He turned around, and again, Joe yelled directly at the Judge. "I want my right to a speedy trial, and I want it now, right now," Joe replied without missing a beat. Joe's lawyer sat motionless without saying a word. "Now, right now, I want my trial!" Joe repeated. The prosecutor said, "Your honor, we have a minor problem with giving Mr. Thornton a trial right now, sir." The Judge tipped his head, "And what might that be? Mr. Thornton has requested a speedy trial to which Mr. Thornton is legally entitled. Why can't we give him his trial."

"Well, your honor," stated the prosecutor, stumbling for the right words, "The witnesses whom Mr. Thornton assaulted are in custody facing attempted murder charges in another district at this time and are not available to us at trial, so we have been delaying this until ...." The Judge stops him from speaking. "Are you kidding," he gasps. The Judge now had a severe problem as the case must be dismissed if the Judge denies Joe a speedy trial. The Judge leaned back in his chair and uttered, "Case dismissed with prejudice." The prosecutor stood up and began a protest, "but your honor." "Sit down, sir, you know the law as well as I, dismissed with prejudice," which ended the prosecution. The Judge continued, "These charges have been waiting to come before my Court for six months, and now you stand there, sir, and tell me the so-called 'victims' of Mr. Thornton's have been charged and awaiting trial with attempted murder in another jurisdiction. What I find strange, Sir, is that what you have just told me sounds like Mr. Thornton's version of the events that led to this prosecution.

The Judge again addressed Joe. "Sir, if you ever come before me again, I will throw the book at you. Do you understand me? Joe nodded, turned, and walked out of the Judge's chambers. Joe thought to himself as he left the building. That's the mistake I made. I should have gone back into the house, grabbed a book, and waved the book over my head at the people with the bats and clubs. The images of the outcome of waving the book filled Joe's head. No, the rifle was the right choice, the rifle. His thoughts continued that we should pass a law that before anyone can become a prosecutor or Judge, they must live in a 'real life' community. I'd love to watch one holding a book over their heads to protect their family. It is this mentality that would send social workers into a war zone. Just show them the book, damn it, show them the book! That's how you would get your ass killed, quick.

And then, the Judge threatened to 'throw the book at me.' Joe had seen the books on the shelves in his attorney's office. They were big, but he knew getting hit with one of those books would not be as bad as getting hit with a damn baseball bat. As he continued, he thought there must be some other world these judges and prosecutors live in. Where lollipops are trees and houses are made of gingerbread.

The events of that evening were finally at an end with the simple words, "dismissed with prejudice." At least now Joe and his family could move on to their next adventure of finding a new home, somewhere quiet, peaceful, and without problems. Well, maybe, but looking back, the 'bad shit' was just about to begin.

CHAPTER SIX

A Farm in Hell

Almost three months have passed since the crazy court ruling dismissing the charges against Joe. On a Tuesday, Barbara told me about Joe finding a farmhouse with some land—a rent-to-purchase deal in the Town of Nassua, in Upstate New York. I could not believe it. Joe and his family would finally have a peaceful, uneventful life as farmers in a rural community. A farm that would be away from the crazy neighbors and all the drama city life had brought to the family. Peace, quiet, paradise, with no neighbors, no issues, be a farmer. I was jealous. My brother Joe had found a place away from it all and a rent-to-buy deal. The best part was the location, only twenty-five miles away, which left the family intact: Brother Joe, the farmer.

Five months had passed since Joe and Barbara moved into their new farm home. Joe and Barbara would visit frequently and inform us of their latest adventures of purchasing animals for the farm and other changes to their lives. And Barbara was now pregnant with their third child, and everything looked up for Joe and Barbara. Looking back, we should have been looking down, down deep as to where the farm was sitting. No one knew then that the farm was less than five hundred feet from a chemical landfill, with things hiding that crept in the water and soil in the night. No one knew, or should I say, if someone did know, no one would speak about it. Nothing about what lurked a few hundred feet from Joe's doorstep!

The first distress call came from Joe in the late afternoon of the spring of nineteen-eighty. "Hello, John, we need you. Can you come here tomorrow," was all Joe said. That is all that needed to be said. After all, he is family, and I would be there as requested.

Early the following morning, I drove along a narrow country road. Mead Road, it said on a sign at the beginning of the road, only one sign, Mead Road. Joe told me to avoid looking for an address as the road only had four houses. His farm was either the first or the last, depending on what end of Mead Road you started on. I looked for Joe's car in the driveway as I passed the first farm. Not seeing Joe's car, I continued to the other end of Mead Road. I found the last farm on the road, and Joe had parked his car right in front. I pulled in behind Joe's car and glanced around. The two-story blue house stood off to the left of where I was parked. Across the driveway was a fair-sized barn with the doors needing repair. On the other side of Mead Road was a fenced-in field, and a single horse was wandering around looking for something to eat. I then noticed a pond to the rear left of the barn sitting about twenty feet and a single duck walking along the shore. I had arrived, yes arrived, at the farm or should I say Joe's home as he requested. I paused for a second, wondering what could be wrong with a pretty farm like this that made Joe place what sounded like a distress call. Well, I wasn't going to find out sitting there, and I opened the door and slid out of the car.

The front door opened directly into the kitchen area of the house. Off to the left was a large living room and a bathroom down a short hallway near the stairs leading upstairs. As expected, Barbara kept the house spotless, and removing shoes was a must to enter.

Joe and Barbara were there to greet me, and the conversation got right down to business. "This is a great little farm," I commented. "How many acres is it?" followed by "How many animals do you now have," I spoke the entire sentences in one breath. Joe responded, "About five acres, counting the fenced-in area across the street, and as far as animals, hard to say they are dropping quickly." I took a second to comprehend what Joe had just said, "what do you mean they are dropping quickly?" The words just flowed from my lips without thought. Joe dropped his head before replying, "Since we have been stocking the farm, the animals just die." He paused, "Pigs found dead, ducks dead next to the pond, geese also dead, and my cow died yesterday. That's when I called you." I interjected, "Have you called a vet and had the farm checked out for problems ......," I was at a loss and did not know what else to suggest. After all, I was a city boy. Barbara chirped, "Well, I called the county, and they sent a man out to check the well water and pond." I responded, "Well, what did they say?" "Say, it's not what they said; it is what they did," Barbara's words were quick, not holding back her emotions. "The man came here, got out of his car, put on a hazmat suit and breathing mask, went down, and took samples of the pond and well water. I confronted him about what he was doing, and his answer was, "I need to be careful here, lady." She continued, "I screamed at this guy. We don't have these space suits, and we live here. What is going on?" The man moved the mask slightly to speak, "I am only here to take the samples. Call the state health department if you need more information about this farm. Sorry, have a good day." With that said, the man went to his car, removed the suit, and left Barbara standing in the driveway. I sat back in my chair and tried comprehending what Barbara had just told me. A man testing water in a hazmat suit did not seem reasonable. I tried to correct Barbara, "You mean he was wearing a white suit, don't you?" "No!" Barbara replied. "It was a damn space suit you see on the news with air breathers and everything." I stood up and walked over to the window to think for a moment, paused, and turned.

I walked back over to a kitchen chair and sat down. Why would people whose job was to guard the health of the general public test water in a hazmat suit? Nothing made sense, and Joe called me to make sense of it. But where do you start? My mother always told us shit slides downhill, and since we were looking for the source of the shit, well, Joe and I were going to go up to the top of the hill, I noticed when I arrived just east of the farm.

The hill was steep, and Joe and I stayed on the roadway to make walking easier. When we arrived at the top of the large hill, we found a chain link fence surrounding a large, overgrown land area. A single sign read, "Private Property – Keep Out," was the only identifier that someone owned the land. A large gate was secured closed by a chain, and the padlock restricted entry, but I noticed the padlock was not rusty and had shown signs of being used recently. Another piece of the puzzle? It was a fenced-in property, no names anywhere to be found, and a lock recently opened. Whatever we were looking for was behind the gated fence, and that is where Joe and I would go.

Joe pulled the bottom of the gate, and an opening large enough formed for us to squeeze through. Once inside, it felt like we were standing in a no-mans-land. Most of the overgrown weeds were still dead from the last winter, but I managed to find several sharp thorn bushes to tear at my skin as we traveled. We noticed tire tracks making lines and knocking down the weeds as they went. The tire tracks seemed recently made by a large truck. I stopped, "Joe, didn't you tell me tanker trucks came down your road in the middle of the night?" Joe paused, tilting his head, "Not a lot, maybe once a week, always after midnight." "I think we have found where they were heading, right here," I said as I continued our walk. We now had an idea where the trucks were heading. The next question is what they did after midnight in an empty-looking, weed-covered area.

We moved another hundred feet into the wasteland and spotted fifty-five-gallon drums painted bright orange, rusted partially, leaking orange goo. I stopped moving to give my nose time to sense the air around us and took a deep breath. "Pesticides, pesticides," I yelled at Joe. "Holy shit," followed. "We are standing in the middle of a chemical dump!" Once again, my mother was right, shit flows downhill, and this shit was some of the bad shit she warned us to stay away from. We stood for a minute and surveyed the area. Drums half sticking out of the ground for as far as we could see covered the entire area. I told Joe, "They dumped the drums just far enough back from the fence so a passerby could not see them. I directed Joe to look at what seemed to be some pipes with caps sticking out of the ground. I pointed and spoke, "Look, Joe, those tankers coming here in the middle of the night are likely dumping waste oil into underground tanks attached to those pipes."

As Joe and I made our way out of the dangerous place, we evaluated what we had found during our travels through hell. The dump site was about sixteen acres in size. That would be three times the size of Joe's farm. It was sitting on top of a hill surrounded by a chain link fence, and according to Joe, trucks were going there in the middle of the night, dumping whatever contents they had onboard with dairy farms surrounding it. The unrusted lock and current tire tracks now made sense, as someone was still using the dump to dispose of waste. As we reached the farmhouse and sat at the kitchen table, I tried to summarize our adventure. "Let's see," I started. "Chemicals of some type are dumped into a site on top of a hill. The water from rain slowly flows down the hill from the area and pollutes the ponds and streams. Animals and dairy cows drink the water and become infected with the chemicals, eventually killing them. People drink the milk from the cows and eat the meat from the other animals and may become sick or worse. Other than that, what could go wrong." I concluded.

We now knew the secret that no one wanted to speak about. A secret was so sinister that it could kill animals and likely people. Well, damn it, somebody knew, and as Joe and I sat at his kitchen table, we vowed to find out who that somebody was. One thing kept repeating itself in the back of my mind. How did the person who owned and rented the farm to Joe, Allan Smith, not know? He farmed and lived here for years. How could he not have known about the dump and not told Joe when he rented the farm? In plain view, the chemical dump sat only five hundred feet from the farm atop a hill. How could Smith not have known? The answer had to be that Allan Smith knew and, like everyone else, said nothing!

While sitting in Joe's kitchen, the questions were flying back and forth. That is when Joe told me about the man from the New York State Agriculture and Markets who met with Joe to discuss the problems with the dying animals. "What did he tell you," I asked. "He told me I was a bad farmer and the animals dying were caused by my not caring for them properly," Joe replied. "Who was this guy," I asked. Joe went over to the kitchen counter and searched for something. Joe stopped looking and grabbed something. The man's card was now in Joe's hand.

I took the card and studied it closely. "So, you are a bad farmer, are you?" repeating the explanation for the animals dying. "Well, maybe it is time to accept that answer and do something about it," was my follow-up. I picked up the telephone and dialed the number on the card. "Hello," echoed in the earpiece of the phone. "Mr. Reams, Mr. Reams of the Ag and Markets of New York," I said. "Well, yes, and who is this," came the reply. "This is John Thornton, and I am at Joe Thornton's farm in Nassua, down on Mead Road. You were here about two weeks ago." I waited for him to recall his visit to the farm. "We just wanted to tell you Joe thinks you are correct about why the animals are dying, and tomorrow morning, they will be loaded into his truck and taken to market." One long sentence, not giving him time to interrupt. There was a long pause followed by, "You can't do that, no you can't do that," he repeated. "Why sure we can," I responded. "Joe's a farmer, and he is going to take what he has produced to market tomorrow!" was my answer. "You don't understand, you can't do that, uh, no, no, you can't," I interrupted, "Of course we can, and tomorrow we will!" He would not give up on Joe taking the animals to market. "I can come out there maybe in a week or two to talk about it," I stopped him right there, "No, tomorrow they go to market! His last words were, "I will be there in one hour to speak with you and Joe. Please wait, and don't do anything, please." The telephone conversation ended abruptly, and the wait began.

The car marked State Of New York arrived just after three PM. A man stepped out, identified himself as Mr.

Reams, and handed me another card. I spoke before he could push any crap our way, "The shit is over, friend. What is happening with this farm, and what is on top of that hill right there." Mr. Reams briefly stood like a deer in the headlights before speaking. "On top of the hill is the Dewey Loeffel Landfill that closed in the early seventies. The State and local governments advised us everything was secure and nothing could leak out. I am unsure, but I do as I am told and go along with whatever policy the administrators lay down. The animals may have died from something from the dump, but chemical poisoning is hard to prove without the livers and other parts of the animals. We tell people it is just bad farming." Joe speaks up, "Well, you're in luck. I have many of the parts you need from the animals that died in my freezer, and I want them tested, and I mean now!"

John stepped back and spoke slowly, "First of all, trucks have been making night runs into the dump to unload as late as last week, So the bullshit of it being closed is just that, bullshit. Next, I realize that helping Joe may cause a problem for you and the administration. I think a better way is for my friends over at News Channel Six to put all of this on the air, and I will be more than happy to present to them how you and your 'higher ups' covered this whole thing up, possibly got people killed, maybe cause cancer, to their children, don't you think, that is a better idea?" Mr. Reams' face was pale as he spoke, "No, you don't need to do that. I will help you. Please, no TV news."

Mr. Reams left with the frozen samples. With the deal, the results would not go to his office but directly to Joe.

Doing the process this way would insulate Mr. Reams from direct knowledge of the results, giving him a 'plausible denial' of what was happening at the site. The bottom line was that Mr. Reams could honestly state, "I never saw those reports or the results."

While waiting for the lab's animal test results, Joe and I researched the dump site and what it might contain. We wrote a warning letter to the Troy Record Newspaper public interest section. The letter was the first of our efforts to sound the warning, a warning no one wanted to hear.

Reprinted here is part of the original letter Joe wrote and submitted to the Troy Record Newspaper for publication. It was titled "THE MISSING PCB's." The letter details the issues with the dump site and how it was contaminating Nassau Lake. It further described the efforts to drill wells over 200 feet deep with steel casings to prevent the well from benzene contamination. It included the death of livestock and the butcher's findings of severe issues with the dead animal's liver. All of the information to sound the alarm of the poisons leaking out of the dump site. The next to last paragraph of the letter states, "I now have a farm with livestock that I cannot eat or sell, and the Health Department still insists, 'THERE IS NOTHING TO WORRY ABOUT.'

THE MISSING PCB's

Last summer the town of Nassau held a town meeting to discuss the problem of the PCB's in Nassau Lake. This problem, according to officials, was caused by the seepage from a local "oil" dump from which the chemicals flowed downstream into the lake. When residents questioned officials about the chance of these chemicals being found in private water supplies, they were assured that the problem was confined to only one well. The well they were talking about is located on the property that I rent from Allen Smith, located on Mead Rd.

Prior to my moving in, Mr. Smith had the well drilled to a depth of over 200 ft. and installed a steel casing and seal to prevent the reoccurrence of chemicals in the well. First tests of samples from the well showed traces of benzene. The Department of Health said this was caused by water remaining from the first well. A test taken shortly afterward proved very promising in that no chemicals were found.

During the months following this second testing my family bathed and drank the well water, feeling quite safe about the well and the water it contained. Questions first appeared when the water I was boiling on the stove caught fire in the pan.

As if this weren't enough! Animals I took to be butchered were found to have bad livers and hearts. That fact, till this day, scares the hell out of me, considering the animals were only six months old!

Upon having this information, I notified the Rensselaer County Health Dept. and told them of the butcher's findings. Mr. John Sheehan from the Health Department came out and took a water sample and also the liver from the butchered pig. These tests took about two months.

The results from the water test showed traces of benzene below the state guidelines for contamination. The result from the liver test showed traces of PCB's also at what they called an acceptable level.

Since that time I have suffered an unusual loss of my livestock. No one seemed interested in the animals that remained until I told them that I sold them to supplement my income.

Mr. Sheehan finally, on Jan. 25,1981, took four chickens to be tested by Agriculture and Markets. These tests were returned in a matter of days. The chickens which were on my farm for seven months were above the tolerance allowed for PCB's. Mr. Ferrard from Agriculture and Markets instructed us not to sell the chickens or their eggs because of the amount of PCB's found. The remaining animals we could sell as long as the prospective buyer was told that the animals might contain PCB's.

In my opinion, the government agencies assigned to protect the health and welfare of the community and state have fallen far short of their responsibilities. The problems that I have encountered have been life shattering. I now have a farm with livestock that I cannot eat or sell, and the Health Department still insists, "THERE IS NOTHING TO WORRY ABOUT."

If you too believe that there is nothing to worry about, then go on about your everyday business. Just remember I also believed that there was nothing to worry about.

Joseph Thornton
BOX 168 MEAD RD
NASSAU NY 12123

Copy of the Original Letter Submitted to the Troy Record Newspaper in 1980

I called it a day after submitting the letter and reviewing our uncovered information. It was late in the afternoon when I left the farm to return to my home. I knew we had missed something and needed to stop and figure out what it was. The figuring ended at around midnight. I sat up in bed and stared at the wall, "someone must have gotten sick or died from that shit, someone," I thought. And if that happened, how would it be tracked or recorded? I envisioned it in my head records must exist somewhere. At that point, I realized records of strange deaths must be somewhere and, until now, somewhere kept out of sight away from prying eyes. Healthy people don't just drop dead; who would want to track these occurrences if they do? Insurance companies would be concerned if their insured started dropping like flies. If it deals with health, why not go to the Health Department and see what they have filed away? That's it. Joe and I would raid the Health Department unannounced and see what they had socked away.

The next day, I arrived at Joe's farm around eleven AM to advise him of my hair-brained plan. "It will be easy," I said. "All we are going to do is go down to the county health department and request to see all the records related to the landfill site, and they will gladly give them to us." Joe responded, "Why would they just give us things we know they want to hide?" That was a damn good question, and I was unsure of an answer and did not answer him, but we went to the health department anyway. I would figure out the stumbling blocks as needed, I hoped.

Our destination was The County Health Department in Troy, New York. The trip was about a half-hour drive from the farm. We arrived at the Health Department office at lunchtime, which was good fortune for us. We opened the door and walked into an office with no one at the reception desk. After making some noise, a woman came out of a rear office area, "may I help you," was her greeting. I said, "We would like your records concerning the Dewey Loeffel Landfill in Nassau." The woman frowned, "I am sorry, but to review the Health Department's public records, all requests to review said records must be in writing, submitted, and approved by my superior." I then asked, "Where is your superior?" "He is eating lunch in the back office," she replied. I smiled, "Great," grabbed a piece of paper on the desk and wrote, "I would like to view all public records dealing with the Dewey Loeffel Landfill in Nassau," and signed it.

After a slight protest, she took the signed paper and left through the door where she entered. She returned shortly with an overweight man in tow. I could tell by the expression on his face that he was not happy we interrupted his lunch. From what I could see, it would be beneficial if he missed a lunch or two. After all, he worked for the Health Department. He answered quickly, "No, you cannot see any records. No, leave." My reply was just as quick, "Okay, I am calling News Center Six, and you can explain why you are denying access to public records. We'll be right back with the media." The man snapped back, "You son of a bitch, okay, you can see the records, you can see all the records, but no one is going to help you find anything you are looking for. "Mrs. Jones, let them in the file room, and that's it, now smart ass, see how far that gets you, smartass!" With that final outburst, the man left, and Mrs. Jones unlocked a door to the file room.

The file room was more significant than I had expected. We needed to determine what to look for or if it even existed. My mom helped out again, "Just start at the beginning," that's what she would say, but she never pointed to the beginning. Joe looked at me, and I looked back at Joe. Okay, so where is the beginning? Let's see if you wanted to put something where no one would probably find it, where would that be? We decided to start in the middle of the room and work our way out in both directions. I told Joe, "Check the first folder in each drawer and the last folder in the drawer. Lastly, pull a center folder out of the drawer. If none of the selected three folders appear connected or reference the Landfill, move on to the next file drawer." As crazy as this method sounds, we narrowed the files to four cabinets in about ten minutes. Four file cabinets loaded with some of the most unbelievable accounts of chemical poisoning imaginable concerning the Landfill, all sitting out of sight in these cabinets.

We found what we were looking for, and now what? We could not just take the documents and leave, which would surely lead to problems. As we turned around, we saw the answer sitting in the corner of the room. The large letters seemed to glow, calling out to Joe and me, XEROX!

As I handed Joe the documents, he hesitated, "John, they did not tell us we could use the copier," he said. I replied, "They didn't tell us we couldn't use it either, did they?" Joe nodded his head and started making copies. The copies contained images and words of cancer caused by chemicals, fish with PCB levels thousands of times the allowable limits, and well tests showing Benzine and pesticides. The substances had migrated from the Landfill for miles, poisoning drinking water, wildlife, livestock, and soil, and even ending up in Nassua Lake. In the cabinets were reports of PCBs found in the milk of dairy cows and other products. Each document related a horror story, and these horrors were all hidden away in these cabinets.

The pile of papers was beginning to grow on the table next to the copier. We had made hundreds of copies of what we thought were the worst things in the files, but we were running out of time. It would soon be that Mrs. Jones or her superior, Mr. Fatso, would check on us. We knew we only had a small portion of what the files contained, but we also knew our limited ability to get the copies out undetected. Closing up the cabinets, we began packing the copies inside our jackets. We hoped Mrs. Jones would not notice how much weight we had gained in the short time we were in the file room. We peered out the file room door, and luck was with us. The reception desk and area still needed someone with the authority to stop us. Joe and I made our way to the exit door, Joe first, and as I passed through the door, I yelled, "Thank you for all of your help," closing the door behind me. I was unsure if we broke any laws by making copies of the documents. But, I was sure we now had the proof, the missing link, you might say, to the mystery of what was killing Joe's animals. Of more significant concern now was the health of Joe's family and all the other unaware residents living in the landfill area and Nassau Lake.

The clock ticked, and the poisons continued to creep out of the dump slowly. Dairies downstream continued to serve the cow's contaminated water and sell the milk they produced to the surrounding communities. Lake Nassua was slowly soaked with PCBs and pesticides and absorbed by the fish. Unsuspecting consumers were eating the 'fresh fish' they believed were wholesome food. And while all this was happening, 'the government, the fiddler continued to play on echoing the all is great song of the day.' Our next move would be to make all we found in the documents public, but how would we do it? We realized there were going to be many unhappy people. We realized families were at stake and knew we had to go forward. We had stepped right into the 'bad shit' mom warned us about, and we were up to our necks and needed air to breathe.

CHAPTER SEVEN

Who Would Listen

The meeting at Nassua Lake started with the usual crap of increasing patronage in using the commercial facilities at the lake. The highlights included advertising the fantastic fishing, boating, and swimming. Joe was in attendance with a small sample of the documents rescued from the Health Department. Joe said he wanted to speak with the committee and the gathering about his concerns about the "possibility of chemicals contaminating the lake and fish originating at the landfill." The head of the committee challenged Joe with spreading falsehoods about mythical chemicals and other toxins coming from a source that government officials had thoroughly discredited. After a heated discussion, Joe was not allowed to present the documents with him that night, and he felt threatened with arrest should he keep making these alleged false claims, damaging the businesses at the lake. As Joe sat patiently, he thought he could hear the sounds of hammers. They were driving the nails deep into the gallows out back of the building. The gallows, should he say another word, would be used to hang him and Barbara.

The meeting soon ended with everyone's head still buried in the sand, Joe's warning unheard. As of this writing, I believe many of the people in attendance that night have died of cancer caused by the phantom chemicals documented in Joe's papers, the papers he was not allowed to present that night. The government officials had won the battle that evening, but the war was beginning, and Brother John was standing by waiting to lock and load the big guns.

The lab test results arrived from the Department of Ag and Markets two days after the meeting at Nassua Lake. I returned to Joe's farm to review or figure out what these reports contained. Upon review, we did not know the chemical lists or if they were dangerous. We did recognize some of them: PCBs thousands of times above the allowable limit, pesticides, no allowable limit but plenty in the water, Benzene, Xylenes, Toluene, and petroleum products—many of the chemicals listed on the report at very high levels.

```
8/80                    NEW YORK STATE DEPARTMENT OF HEALTH
                        DIVISION OF LABORATORIES AND RESEARCH
                          ENVIRONMENTAL HEALTH CENTER

                          RESULTS OF EXAMINATION
                               (PAGE 1 OF 1)
LAB ACCESSION NO: 80961   YR/MO/DAY/HR SAMPLE REC'D: 80/07/14/13

REPORTING LAB: 1/ EHC ALBANY
PROGRAM: 136 TOXIC SUBST. MGT.
STATION (SOURCE) NO:
DRAINAGE BASIN: 13 NY GAZETTEER NO: 4155 COUNTY: RENSSELAER
COORDINATES:    DEG  '  "N.    DEG  '  "W
COMMON NAME INCL SUBW'SHED: ALAN SMITH PROPERTY JOE THORNTON RES HEAD RD
                           NASSAU
EXACT SAMPLING POINT: KIT TAP
TYPE OF SAMPLE: 12 WATER, DRILLED WELL
MO/DAY/HR OF SAMPLING: FROM 00/00 TO 07/14/12
REPORT SENT TO: CO (1) RU (1) LPHE (1) LHO (0) FED (0) CHEM (1)
```

Header Page of The Report Received by Joe Thornton

While Joe and I were reading the report and attempting to figure out what it all meant, Barbara pipes up, "That explains why the water caught fire on the stove." I slowly turned my head towards Barbara. "What did you just say?" I asked. "One day, the water boiling on the stove caught fire, and I had to wait for it to burn itself out," Barbara repeated. She continued, "The worst part is I need to keep coloring my hair as the water in the shower turns it orange." Why these pieces of information did not seem important to Barbara escapes me. She later told me she wrote them down somewhere on a piece of paper but forgot to give the paper to me. Still, she believed the information about the water catching fire was included in the article that the Newspaper rejected, and I just missed it.

There was no more time to delay, and the people 'in charge' were determined to keep this information as quiet as possible. The information needed to get out and get out now. Joe had tried a town meeting but failed, and they attempted to make him out a fool. It was time for the nuclear option. I picked up the telephone, dialed

New Center Six, and spoke with an investigative reporter named Jack Aernecke.

Mr. Aernecke listened patiently, but I doubt he believed a word I was saying. "I know this sounds crazy," I said. "Water had caught fire on the stove, animals are dying, I have Health Department documents showing people have been chemically poisoned, ...," I continued. "Hold it," echoed back from the phone. "You have Health Department documents showing what?" Mr. Aernecke said. "I have personally tried to investigate the Dewey Loeffel Landfill and contacted New York State and other local agencies requesting information. According to them, no reports or other documents are anywhere to be found. Would you please repeat what you just told me about documents?" "Sure," I replied. "My brother Joe and I went to the Health Department, and I guess you would say, 'removed copies of records without them knowing it; I guess you could say we robbed the Health Department' concerning the landfill." The telephone went dead for a few seconds, "We will be at your place in an hour. Have the documents. We want to see them." The conversation ended that quickly, and the wait began for the news crew. We finally had someone's attention, and that person's voice would be heard as far away as Washington, D.C.

The news crew and Mr. Aernecke arrive right on schedule. His first words were, "May I see the documents?" I handed over a small pile of papers stamped with the Health Department seal, dated on the received date, and signed for. He laid the papers on a table and instructed the cameraman to take a "shot" of the documents Mr. Aernecke was told did not exist. He wanted to hear the story about the trip to the Health Department and how we figured out where the documents had been 'misplaced' in the files. "Strange," he commented. "I have tried for years to get a hold of documents like these and for years told they do not exist. It required two guys with big balls to walk in the front door and take them. Just unbelievable!"

The next night, the lead story on the Six O'clock News was "The Dewey Loeffle Landfill – Poisoning the Town of Nassua Lake. Documents reveal what appears to be a coverup at the State and local levels!" The newscast ended with, "The investigation will continue as new evidence is revealed!" I called Joe after seeing the news and commented, "I think the cat is out of the bag!"

Now that Joe had the proof that the landfill was the likely cause, things began to move forward very fast. New York State, the Fed, Local government, everybody was there drilling, digging, pouring cement walls, you name it, they did it to stop the chemicals from leaking out of the site. To sum up what happened, they all got caught minimizing the risk from the chemical landfill, and now they needed to blame someone else for the coverup. What was more interesting was that when other people returned to the Health Department looking for documents, they were not to be found. Even the papers Joe and I had made copies of were now missing. It was never adequately explained how two guys with big balls had copies of stamped documents that a government agency says do not exist. When the government gets involved, to quote Lewis Carroll's 'Alice in Wonderland,' things keep getting curiouser and curiouser!

News agencies and newspapers swarmed Joe's farm and the Nassua Lake area within a day. A small sample of what the media reported: One Newspaper states: "The fall of Nassau Lake .... *Now, they say, the lake is a 'disaster.'*

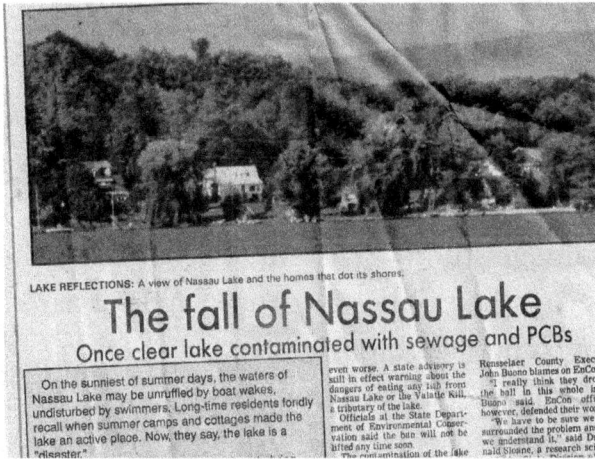

The fall of Nassau Lake
Once clear lake contaminated with sewage and PCBs

LAKE REFLECTIONS: A view of Nassau Lake and the homes that dot its shores.

On the sunniest of summer days, the waters of Nassau Lake may be unruffled by boat wakes, undisturbed by swimmers. Long-time residents fondly recall when summer camps and cottages made the lake an active place. Now, they say, the lake is a "disaster."

even worse. A state advisory is still in effect warning about the dangers of eating any fish from Nassau Lake or the Valatie Kill, a tributary of the lake.

Officials at the State Department of Environmental Conservation said the ban will not be lifted any time soon.

The contamination of the lake

Rensselaer County Execu John Buono blames on EnCon

"I really think they drop the ball in this whole iss Buono said. EnCon offic however, defended their wor

"We have to be sure we surrounded the problem and we understand it," said Dr. nald Sloane, a research scie

Old Local Newspapers Clippings Believed to be From The Troy Record Newspaper

One newspaper article read: "**Total fishing ban in Valatie Kill Extended by Encon.** *The total ban on fishing in the Valatie Kill flowing into Nassau Lake and the partial ban on some species within Nassau Lake itself has been extended... The source of the PCBs is believed to be the former Dewey Loeffel waste disposal site in Nassua, says Rensselaer County Health engineer Loren Lutz...*"

Lake pollution update given

By RICHARD CRIST
Record Correspondent

NASSAU — Little has changed at the Dewey Loeffel landfill over the past few years.

State officials are still trying to determine what is causing contamination in Nassau Lake and the nearby Valatie Kill, and residents near the lake and the closed dumpsite are still concerned about falling property values.

Residents got an update on the situation with the landfill, which contains more contaminants than Love Canal, at a forum last night at the Donald P. Southerland School sponsored by a town councilman.

Representatives of the state Department of Environmental Conservation noted that a no-eat order for fish caught in the lake or the kill is still in effect. The no-eat order was issued in 1988.

"Unfortunately, the fish in Nassau Lake are still not suitable for consumption," said Ron Sloan, an analyst with EnCon. Toxic "concentrations in fish are still high," Sloan said.

Contamination in sediment and fish from the lake is still high, estimated at 20 parts per million — 10 times higher than the federally allowed level.

Mead Road, residents concerned with falling property values and other negative effects were urged by a local attorney to check into investigating legal action before statutes of limitation run out.

"The biggest problem I see is that people wait too long," said Albany attorney Salvatore Ferlazzo. "Don't sit on your rights."

Ferlazzo, an attorney with O'Connell and Aronowitz, said that he is preparing legal actions against General Electric for several residents. In addition, a separate claim is being filed against GE by another resident.

Ferlazzo did not say what residents are involved in the suit he is currently preparing.

Residents are still concerned about the effects of the landfill, which was used as a chemical dump by General Electric and Schenectady Chemical throughout the 1950s and 1960s. Dumping at the site was coordinated by resident Dewey Loeffel.

The landfill was remediated and capped in the mid-1980's after legal settlements were reached with General Electric.

"Let's face it, it's nearly ten years after the cleanup, and fish are still contaminated," said Ferlazzo.

Lake Pollution Update

The article quotes: *"Little has changed at the Dewey Loeffel landfill over the past few years. ..... Let's face it's nearly ten years after the cleanup, and fish are still contaminated."*

Joe finally got them to listen! Not long after Joe forced the news into the public view, the EPA designated the site for a superfund cleanup.

EPA Official Document Concerning the Landfill

The Dewey Loeffel Landfill is an in . In the 1950s and 1960s, several companies, including , , and Schenectady Chemicals, used the site as a disposal facility for more than 46,000 tons of industrial hazardous wastes, including solvents, waste oils, (PCBs), scrap materials, sludges, and solids. Some dangerous substances, including (VOCs) and PCBs, have migrated from the facility to underlying aquifers and downstream surface water bodies, contaminating groundwater, surface water, sediments, and several fish species. There is currently a ban on fish consumption in and the impacted tributaries.

Almost thirty years after Joe revealed the dangers the Dump Site represented to the local community, a news

report in April 2019, News 10, ABC channel news reported, "New area of contamination discovered near Nassau
landfill."

The Town of Nassau was recently notified by the United States Environmental Protection Agency (EPA) that
a site on Route 203 in the Town, believed to be related to the Dewey Loeffel operations, had tested positive
for significant contamination. This contamination is approximately 5.5 miles from the federal Dewey Loeffel
Superfund Site.

The previously known contamination at the Dewey
Loeffel Landfill Superfund Site had been a disposal facility for more than 46,000 tons of industrial hazardous
wastes, including solvents, waste oils, PCBs, sludge, and
solids. The contamination is two times the volume of the
infamous Love Canal....

Today, you will find a sign like this standing guard at
the dump site warning of the dangers Joe and I presented
back in nineteen eighty. How many people have become
sick, died, or will die from the poison dumped into the
landfill may never be known.

Hazardous Waste Sign at Dump Site

Again, in 2021, problems emerged around the landfill. A story written by Arin Cotel-Altman of Rensselaer County details the events from a serious storm. The report reads in part:

Intense flooding hit Rensselaer County two weeks ago, and flow gauges for bodies of water like the Valatie Kill went off the charts.

"There hadn't been flow rates at that level even during Tropical Storm Irene," said Nassau Supervisor David Fleming. "So what we had here was a tremendous amount of water flow in a very short period."

Because of the flooding, officials said sediments from the toxic Dewey Loeffel Landfill Superfund site flowed into Little Thunder Brook and the Valatie Kill, two bodies of water near the landfill.

They are concerned that the sediment brought toxins such as polychlorinated biphenyls (PCBs). The U.S. Environmental Protection Agency (EPA) collected surface water and sediment samples from residential properties.

What You Need To Know

Because of flooding two weeks ago, sediments from the toxic Dewey Loeffel Landfill Superfund site have entered Little Thunder Brook and the Valatie Kill.

There are concerns that this sediment brought toxins like PCB's

The EPA is testing surface water samples and sediment deposits on residential properties.

"We're obviously interested to see the test results on the surface water," Fleming said. "But right now, our main focus is sediment because many PCBs cling to sediment. So folks from the landfill down through the village of Nassau are having their properties tested."

The Dewey Loeffel Landfill served as a dump site in the 1950s and 1960s and was declared a Superfund site decades later due to the presence of PCBs and 1,4-dioxane, a potential cancer-causing contaminant.

Fleming says the EPA will be collecting samples through July 30, so anyone who wants testing done on sediment deposits on their property should contact them.

"If you have a yard where there are sediment deposits and things, I strongly urge you to keep your pets away, keep your kids away until those test results are back from the EPA.

CHAPTER EIGHT

Escape From Hell

M aking the information public to protect others did not make him any friends, and the value of the farm was about zero after all the news reports. Even more impressive was the number of people who refused to believe the Dump Site was dangerous to the community. People living in Nassua would drive down Mead Road to evaluate the issue as if seeing it would change the reality of the chemicals leaking from the site. Some passers-by would stop at the chained gate at the Dump Site and stare into the overgrown area, declaring they could see no problem at the site and the news was blowing the trouble out of proportion. Many people driving by pointed to Joe's house almost accusingly; if not for him, no problems would exist. Everything would be fine if not for what Joe had done by going to the media with a false story about demons lurking in the ground.

Our mother had it right when she said, "People will believe what they are willing to accept as true, and they will not let the facts stand in their way." What other people were willing to believe did not change Joe's position. His problem now was, what do you do with a farm, five hundred feet from a chemical landfill, and leaking poisons? He had spent most of his money on animals that had died or were sick. He now had three children: Christopher, approximately a year old; Spring Bobby Jo, seven; and Joe Jr., almost eleven. The options were minimal based on Joe's resources, but something needed improvement. Joe was not a big fan of lawyers after the events from Phelan Court Apartments, but the events on Mead Road left him without many choices.

A week after the news story broke, Joe, Barbara, and I headed to Albany to find an attorney willing to fight the big corporations and the government and win. Another problem was that we did not know what deals or agreements had been made with the State of New York or the Federal Government concerning the Dump Site. We felt something was going on behind the scenes to allow the cover-up, but we did not know what to expect.

After several stops at different law offices, we were concerned that no lawyer would take on a case of this type. Each attorney we spoke with turned us down, stating the case would be unprovable. It was with the last attorney that I decided to change our approach. Instead of telling a story that was hard to believe, I would start with the Health Department documents.

As we entered the conference room of our last attorney, our hopes of finding a lawyer to take Joe's case were significantly reduced. We slowly circled a large table, sat down, and waited. When the attorney entered the room, we introduced ourselves, and I immediately spread out the 'recovered documents' from the Health Department. "Before we start with the story, here's the proof," I said, moving the papers closer toward him. I did not know if this approach would work, but nothing else worked. Why not give it a try? The attorney looked at the documents before him, "how did you get these papers?" he questioned. As he looked deeper into the records, he looked up at Joe, "Here is a report of a man who died from chemical poisoning by eating the fish in Lake Nassau, and here's a report of the same chemicals that killed the man taken from a sample from the landfill." He shook his head and stepped back from the table before speaking. "And how did you get the Health Department to give these documents to you?" I looked at Joe before commenting, "Well, Sir, we just went in and copied them while they were at lunch." He began to laugh before saying, "You robbed the damn Health Department, now that's funny." He continued. Let me have my partners look at the papers, and I will get back to you shortly.

As we left the attorney's office, we were not sure if we had an attorney, but at least we had a shot at getting one. The answer came two days later in the form of a letter.

The top part of the letter accepting the case follows:

JOHN T. DEGRAFF
WILLIAM F. CONWAY
JOHN E. HOLT-HARRIS, JR
CARROLL J. MEALEY
JOHN T. DEGRAFF, JR
FRANK J. LASCH
FREDERICK C. RIESTER
DAVID F. KUNZ
ALGIRD F. WHITE, JR.
MICHAEL G. BRESLIN
MICHAEL F. DALY
MICHAEL J. CUNNINGHAM
ROBERT H. ISEMAN
MICHAEL T. WALLENDER
TERENCE J. DEVINE

DE GRAFF, FOY, CONWAY, HOLT-HARRIS & MEALEY
ATTORNEYS AND COUNSELORS AT LAW
NINETY STATE STREET
ALBANY, NEW YORK 12207
TELEPHONE (518) 462-5301

GEORGE W. FOY
(1902-1973)

ALDEN C. MERRICK
(1906-1979)

KATHRYN M. LASCH
THOMAS S. WEST
ROBERT H. BIXBY
F. DOUGLAS NOVOTNY
BARBARA S. BRENNER

March 30, 1981

Mr. & Mrs. Joseph Thornton
c/o John Thornton
87 Homewood Avenue
Watervliet, New York

Re: Loeffel Landfill

Dear Mr. & Mrs. Thornton:

I am writing to confirm the substance of my conversation

A few weeks later, the story about the lawsuit broke in a local newspaper. Named as defendants are Allan Smith, the owner of the farm property; Bendix Corp.; General Electric; and Schenectady Chemicals, the parties that either dumped the material or paid someone to leave it on their behalf.

Couple files $33 million lawsuit in landfill case

By PHIL BROWN
Staff Reporter

NASSAU — A Rensselaer County couple has filed a $33 million lawsuit against General Electric, Schenectady Chemicals and Bendix Corp. for dumping toxic chemicals in the Dewey Loeffel landfill in the Town of Nassau in the 1960s.

In the lawsuit, Joseph and Barbara Thornton claim they and their three children suf...

McGinn said the Thorntons are "mostly concerned" about their one-year-old son, Christopher, who was born while they lived at the farm.

General Electric, Schenectady Chemicals and Bendix deposited 46,320 tons of toxic chemicals at the landfill from 1952 to 1970, when the dumping stopped, according to state Department of Environmental Conservation officials. In May 1980, EnCon identified the landfill as the source of PCBs found in fish from the Valatie Kill and Nassau Lake.

complaint. "When I rented (the farm) to him, the health department approved it," marked Smith, a dairy farmer.

General Electric and Bendix have agreed to pay their share of cleaning up the landfill, the state attorney general had to file a lawsuit against Schenectady Chemicals to tempt to force that company to assume some of the expense.

General Electric, which admitted responsibility for percent of the wastes dumped at the site, has hired Syracuse engineering firm to design walls and covering...

$33 Million Dollar Lawsuit Filed

The lawsuit would be complex and challenging to win against the three large corporations who defended their actions. Their defense was simple: 'They did not dump it there.' See the person we paid to take it away. What made the lawsuit even more difficult was that each company had an agreement with the State of New York to shield them from individual liability. Going to see the company that operated the dump site as suggested by the defendants was impossible, a fact they readily understood. Of course, that person was the owner of the dump site who shut it down many years before and went out of business. The owner of the property, Allan Smith, his only asset was the farm contaminated with poison. Why would anyone want it, as it was unlivable being so close to the Dump Site?

The case was never going to see its day in Court. The corporations responsible for the contamination each either had or were in the process of making a deal with New York State. The Court restricted Joe's attorneys by prior deals with the State of New York or other agreements with the corporations limiting individual rights to sue for damages caused by their chemicals.

The only leverage Joe's attorney had was the documents showing the effort to cover up the issues at the dump. Because of these 'non-existent documents, ' the Defendant offered a settlement to Joe and Barbara. The only payments Joe and Barbara received were enough funds to move and place a down payment on another piece of property. Although I cannot disclose the exact amount of the payments or other terms of the agreement, they totaled less than thirty thousand dollars. As for the copies of the documents taken from the County Health Department by Joe and me, the settlement required the attorney to retain them and not return them to Joe and Barbara Thornton. Like many of the documents concerning the Dewey Loeffel Site, these records have been mislaid and lost to eternity and are no longer available. After all, according to officials, they never existed in the first place!

Follow Up Notes

Readers should also note that over the last forty years, each of the three large corporations has paid large sums of money to the government to help clean up the landfill and even built a water treatment plant at the site. Unfortunately, the landfill, even today, continues to leak the poisons into the water and has contaminated large amounts of property, now miles away from the site where the dumping occurred.

One final note: as a significant contributor of the contaminated wastes, approximately 37,530 tons, GE was ordered to remove 500 surface drums and four 30,000-gallon oil storage tanks from the site in the 1980s as part of a broader agreement with the New York State Department of Environmental Conservation (NYSDEC). They [GE and responsible parties] had the opportunity before the landfill was capped and reburied to provide a complete remediation, removing the toxins from the site.

For decades, the town of Nassau has been trying to get a health study related to the impacts of the Dewey Loeffel Site, and that has yet to happen based on several excuses from different agencies. To this day, government officials still block the town of Nassau from discovering the total extent of damage caused by the landfill.

Unable to get an official study, residents of the town, along with the citizen advisory group UNCAGED (United Neighbors Concerned about General Electric and the Dewey Loeffel Landfill), put together a health survey that went out to residents in the affected areas in the 1990s. They created a pushpin map to document the results. What came about from that mapping was that there were clusters of cancer directly related to the Dewey Loeffel Landfill and the contamination it contained.

The owner of the farm rented to Joe and Barbara, Allan Smith, is believed to have died in his early fifties from cancer.

CHAPTER NINE

Buying The Farm

The nightly news reports concerning the Dump Site were getting more detailed daily. The State of New York was at the forefront, beating its chest and laying down the law about what it would accomplish. The hazmat suit people spent their time working with large drilling equipment at the Dump Site. Federal officials were constantly coming and inspecting whatever work others had completed, and of course, the media was right there to record the events for the nightly news.

The politicians pointed fingers and blamed everyone else but themselves. They constantly repeated, "If I were informed about what was happening at the Dump Site, I would have put my foot down and not allowed it to happen. Please vote for me to avoid issues like this in the future." The amount of 'gaslighting' being presented could have fueled a power plant.

The entire chain of events that led up to what was now happening at the Dump Site would have been like a circus if the consequences had not been so severe. I, for one, was dumbfounded as to how many people still believed that just letting the stuff sit there was the solution to the problem, as it would disappear.

While all these events moved forward, my Brother Joe thought about his next move while sitting in his Hess station office. Twenty-eight miles, twenty-eight miles, Joe thought. Is that far enough away from the Dewey Loeffel Landfill? Another thought was if he was far enough away from all the people at Nassua Lake, convinced he caused the entire problem. To be sure, he repeated in his head, Nassau, New York, to Pittstown, New York, twenty-eight miles. He smiled; that must be far enough away from that nasty shit; that has to be far enough, and with that reasoned out, Joe decided where his new home/farm was going to be. Twenty-eight miles from the hell on earth the landfill was unleashing. Twenty-eight long miles, with no chemicals, no nosey neighbors, nothing but my land to raise my family and build a home, twenty-eight long miles. He sat there and smiled; no more dangers, he thought to himself, paradise at last. With his feet on top of his desk, Joe leaned back to figure out how he would make this move happen and, for a moment, just closed his eyes to dream.

Joe opened his eyes, stalling his dream, and he dialed the telephone. The telephone rang just before noon, and I found Joe on the other end of the phone line. "I found one," were the first words from Joe's mouth. I interrupted, "One, what did you find?" "I found a farm, another farm," replied Joe. I grabbed a chair and sat down, waiting to hear the details. I continued, "Okay, please don't tell me it is in Naussa or anywhere near the landfill," "No, listen, no, it is in Pittstown, fifteen miles outside of Troy and twenty-eight miles from the dump." Joe got all of this sentence out, ensuring there was nowhere for me to interrupt. I said, "Do you have enough money and everything needed to make the move and start over?" After a pause, Joe replied, "That is just like you always thinking down the road. In my world, I do things one step at a time. Step one: I find a place. Step two: get ready to make the move. Step three is to see if we can afford it, and if not. Step four: call you so you can tell us how we can afford it." Joe ended with, "I will call you later," and hung up. I took a moment to think over what Joe had just told me and concluded that his reasoning was perfect: dump the problems on your older brother to figure out and move forward; that seemed like an ideal rationale plan.

The next time I spoke with Joe was about three days later. As always, Joe acted with his impulses, met with the realtor, and placed a down payment on the farm in Pittstown. Joe learned the farm owner was willing to hold the mortgage paper, and he and his family could move in whenever they were ready. Ready? Are you kidding? The move started two days later using a rented U-haul truck, a trailer, two cars, and a small group of friends. Goodbye, dumpsite, hello paradise! All that was missing was the parade by the locals at Nassua Lake celebrating Joe's leaving the Nassua Lake area.

The farm in Pittstown, New York, covered five acres and was positioned on a corner lot at the intersection of all the main roads. Here, Joe felt, the three children would be safe and grow up without the challenges of the prior locations. Joe and Barbara spent the first night just sitting on the porch and feeling good about this great move. They were finally home where nothing, no nothing, nothing lurking in the night to endanger them, nothing. Of course, the three children, Joe Jr., eleven years old, Spring Bobby Jo, eight years old, and Christopher, almost two, would love it. The farm spelled adventure to young kids. Joe looked at Barbara, "You know the kids are going to love this place as soon as I can fix it." Joe had never told Barbara how much work the farm needed, but when you buy an old run-down farm, well, you get an old run-down farm.

The farm's layout on the day Joe's family moved in consisted of a central two-story house, painted white, sitting in the corner of the five-acre lot. A yellow, more minor, two-story guest house stood about 100 feet east of the main house. Across the large gravel driveway leading up to the main house stood a huge two-story barn missing the doors. The farm owners had painted the barn brown, but due to the lack of maintenance, most of the brown color had bleached away, leaving the barn gray. Standing in the driveway, you could see most of the remaining five acres overgrown and unmanaged. The main benefit was that it did not have close neighbors or chemicals leaking to sneak up on you in the night. The family was now on its own to sink or swim, and Joe was determined to swim. It would take time, but Joe had time to build a new home and raise a family.

Where do you start when trying to build your family home? Joe laid down on the makeshift bed upstairs, closed his eyes, and drifted off to sleep, leaving this unanswered question for tomorrow.

Joe awoke at four a.m. the following morning. He was startled by the unfamiliar surroundings and took a moment to evaluate where he was. Barbara was still asleep lying next to him, which brought with it some peace that things were okay. Joe slowly moved to the edge of the bed and surveyed his new surroundings. Things looked very different than when they moved in the furniture. The shadows of night changed Joe's perception, and the darkness always allowed the mind to wander, filling in whatever could not be seen clearly. In the dark shadows in an unknown area, a chair could become a wild animal and a hose a vicious snake. He stood up and headed for the only light he could see glowing in the darkness. The single light Barbara had left on showing the way to the bathroom to guide one in a night visit.

Four a.m., shit, four a.m. on a Saturday. Well, I'm up, thought Joe. And now that I am up, what should I do at four a.m. so I don't wake the rest of the house? Joe slipped down the stairs, out the front door, and walked over to the barn and through the missing door. He shined the flashlight he picked up on the way out the door and scanned the empty structure. The barn was a large two-story building with horse stalls and hay loft. Joe began to lay out the needed repairs and thought I could do so many things with this old barn after I had time to replace the missing door. Joe's mind began to race with ideas about what he could do with a barn like this. Like a thief in the night, he moved around using the flashlight, looking for whatever may have been left by the previous owners. The barn lacked valuable treasures besides horseshoes and a piece of chain hanging on the wall. When it came time to fix this old barn, all materials would need to come from somewhere else. Joe stopped as he passed back through the broken barn door; it was hard to believe they didn't even leave a two-by-four to start repairs.

As Joe left the barn, he looked out into what was at one time the field area, now overgrown and needing major work to return it to its glory. He stopped and reviewed in his head what tools and farm equipment they had brought from the Lake Nassau farm. Joe had shovels, gardening equipment, a chainsaw, and other hand tools. His head lifted again, and he looked at the acres of un-managed field before him. "Shit," he said. I am going to need a tractor and a big tractor to boot. Where do I get a tractor, or better yet, where do I get the money for a tractor when I find one?

Joe began to walk back toward the main house, drag-ging his feet through the gravel of the driveway. When Joe returned, he found Barbara moving around the kitchen. The kitchen was a little light on appliances and consisted of a refrigerator, stove to cook on, if it worked, and a sink. The water in the sink did work, but the jury was still out regarding the kitchen stove. They discovered that at least one of the top burners did not light, and after opening the oven door, Joe was afraid to strike a match to check it. While looking into the oven, Joe could hear in the back of his head his mother saying the words, "Bad shit." That was his mother's term for things that could or would go wrong should you do it. Yeah, Joe thought, lighting that oven could be 'bad shit' or maybe even 'really bad shit.' Joe listened to his mother and put the matches back in his pocket. He concluded the kitchen would need some work to make it usable, but first things first.

In Joe's mind, a list was forming: let's see, first, we must get a tractor and then a stove, or rather a stove and then a tractor. Joe deferred to Barbara to decide what should be purchased first: the tractor he wanted or the kitchen stove. Barbara chose the stove as the priority for the home. Joe reminded Barbara that he was the ruler of the roost, and he thought they should buy a tractor first. Joe may have been the ruler, but Barbara was right there to overrule him.

Later that same morning, they left to purchase a new stove in the city. Joe, being the intelligent person Joe is, made it out to Barbara that he would have also decided to put the stove first. As for myself, being Joe's older brother, I'd bet anything, leaving it for Joe to decide; Joe would have been riding the tractor while Barbara cooked over a campfire.

Weeks had passed, and the daily routine was that Joe would go to work at the Hess station he managed, come home, fix things at the house, and go to bed. This work schedule was repeated five days a week, with the weekend reserved for only fixing up something at home. On the other hand, Barbara would clean and move things daily.

One day, she would clean and move things to the right, then clean them and move them left the next day. It took a while, but slowly, Joe and Barbara were converting a run-down farmhouse into a home for the family.

One of the main issues with the renovated farmhouse was how to heat it during the long Upstate New York winters. The original owners had a single propane-fired heating stove in the downstairs living room and electric heaters in the upstairs bedrooms. Joe asked Barbara, "Do you know what that will cost? Propane and electricity are expensive, and we have five acres of wood just laying there for the taking," Barbara nodded before speaking, "But how will we get the wood just laying there over here?" Joe does not want not to have an answer and replies, "It would be easier if we had a tractor, but for now, we will cut it in the field, move it in a wheel barrel, and stack it along the side of the house near the kitchen. Barbara always smiled when Joe figured out a problem; now, it would be no different. As she started to turn away, she stopped. "But what will we use to burn the wood we just gathered?" The question caught Joe by surprise as that had not yet crossed his mind, and he paused before answering, "I will work that out tomorrow," and left the kitchen.

The children helped when they could. Joe Jr., the oldest at eleven, was just like his father in many ways, some good, and some, well, you know what I mean. Let's say he was much like Joe Sr. and leave it there. Spring Bobby Jo, now eight, was a young lady in every way. One would think she would be a 'tomboy' living on a farm with only brothers, and you would be wrong. Christopher, the youngest at almost three, was already too damn smart for his age. Chris could put the 'terrible threes,' as they are called, to shame. There was nothing he would not get into, nor could you hide anything from him. I, for one, was not sure how things would go with the kids on the farm. But I knew Joe would keep them in line. Joe was never mean or nasty, but he meant what he said, and he did not like to repeat himself. Of course, when it came to his children, Joe adjusted the number of times to repeat himself to four. And that is how it went when Joe laid down the law and spoke: He would tell Barbara only once and the kids four times.

CHAPTER TEN

The Guest House

The days turned into weeks, the weeks turned into months, and the months into years. Nothing happens quickly on a farm when you work full-time and try to rebuild the property in your spare time. During this time, Joe had remodeled the guest house and, needing extra money, decided to use it as a rental property. The tiny yellow house with the brown porch was attractive, should be easy to rent, and looked very good when viewed from the street. A small ad in a local publication generated some interest, but the location about fifteen miles from the city made it less than desirable for most. Finally, a single woman named Mary, with her two children, agreed to rent the house. The two-story house was perfect for her and her kids. She commented on how well-kept it was as she did the first walk-through of the guest house. The tiny house had a kitchen, bathroom, and living room downstairs, and the bedrooms upstairs with a second bathroom. For her and her two children, it was perfect. It got her out of the city she hated, and the kids had total access to the local farm and fields. Joe and Mary agreed upon a fair price, and the house was hers to enjoy. The only limitation on the rental was that Mary would not have anyone else living there as Joe was fed up with close neighbors and wanted to avoid future problems. She readily agreed with that limitation, stating she had no one in her life, and it would not be a problem. About two days later, Mary and her two children moved into the guest house, paying the first month's rent.

The Guest House

About four months had passed since the guest house rental, and as agreed, Mary paid the rent on the first of each month without an issue. Mary always paid in cash, claiming something about not trusting banks as they were unsafe. The first hint of a problem occurred in the fifth month: no Mary, no money for the rent. Joe figured she forgot to drop it off and waited until the next month's rent came due. After waiting almost three weeks into the sixth month, Joe realized something was wrong and needed to address whatever it was now. He would need to speak with Mary to see the problem, if any, causing her not to pay the agreed-upon rent.

Joe slowly walked across the wet grassy area between his main house and the rented guest house. The woman tenant was now almost two months late with the rent, and Joe felt he had been more than patient waiting for the rent money. He ascended the small set of steps and knocked on the door. As the door opened, a man stood in the doorway, a man unknown to Joe. "Who are you," Joe asked. "I am Mary's boyfriend, why." Was his quick reply as if that was all the answer required to end the conversation? Moving back slightly from the door, Joe responded, "The agreement I have with Mary is that she and her two children could live here and no one else, which includes 'boyfriends,' and that includes you." "Let me tell you something, buddy," squirted out of the mouth of the boyfriend. "First of all, Mary can have anybody she wants to stay here with her, and I know she is late with the rent, but I know our rights. We do not need to pay the rent for six months before you can file to evict us, and then we have three more months after the finalized paperwork for the court eviction before we need to leave. You got that, buddy, we know our rights!" as the boyfriend slammed the door in Joe's face.

Joe thought as he walked off the porch; okay, have it your way; I guess he knows his rights. Joe's mind drifted back to when he first walked into the attorney's office in Troy about the assault charges from Phelan Apartments. All those books lining the walls of the office, he thought. There must be something in them to help me with this problem. It was then Joe realized how much he hated to read anything, and even thinking about reading all those books would not work. Plan 'B' was needed, and plan 'B' would be easier for Joe to deal with.

Joe once again traveled the path over the grassy area back to the main house. Entering the house, he moved over to the locked gun cabinet, removed the double-barrel shotgun, and pushed two shells into the opened chambers. Joe left the home, stopping in the garage and picking up a few hand tools before returning to address the stranger. Joe arrived at the guest house's front door moments later, prepared to make his case concerning the rent.

Joe knocked, and the door opened. Without saying a word, Joe pushed the stranger back into the house with the shotgun's pointed barrel. Joe presses the gun against the man's chest, walks the man backward against the hallway wall, and then speaks softly and calmly. "I know you know your rights because you told me so, and I respect your rights. But you should have kept reading that bullshit book you got that out of. The book also states, 'Your rights end where mine begin,' and you are at the beginning of mine on the end of this shotgun." Joe continued, "Now let me see what happened here today: Mary was not home, and I heard an intruder in her house, that would be you, pried open a window, that window over there," Joe then dropped the pry bar he picked up in the garage at the man's feet. "And the intruder attacked me with a weapon," Now dropping a small hatchet next to the man also from his garage. "To defend myself, I had to shoot the intruder with my shotgun, killing him. Does that story seem good enough to you, Mr. Intruder?" Joe's speech was direct and to the point. Looking directly into Joe's face, the man could see he meant every word he said. He seemed to agree with the story and took in every word as Joe spoke. Joe stepped back from the man and slowly picked up his dropped tools. "If I need to return here again, I won't need to pick up these tools, do you understand?" Joe spoke these final words before leaving the house, giving the intruder some time to think over what he had said.

Joe returned to his home and replaced the shotgun in the cabinet. The tools the 'intruder' had used to break into the house Joe dropped into their proper location in the garage. Joe then returned to working around the farm to complete his daily chores.

The afternoon moved quickly; it was time for supper around six, and Barbara served the meal she had been preparing for the family. You could hear the noise of people loading furniture and other belongings into a rented trailer parked outside the guest house. Barbara glances out the window before speaking, "Looks like Mary is leaving. I guess she probably couldn't afford the rent and decided to move," Joe chirps in, "No, I spoke with her boyfriend earlier, and he told me he did not want to be an intruder anymore. I guess they decided leaving was the right thing to do before they stepped on my rights." Mary, the two children, and the man/intruder who knew his rights were gone by late evening, leaving the rental house empty and needing more minor repairs.

CHAPTER ELEVEN

Moving Forward

The guest house was to remain empty for the next several months. Joe used this time to go in and again make the needed repairs and updates after their tenant had left, damaging small things in the house as they went. Re-renting the guest house, at least for now, was put on the back burner. There was so much around the farm to complete, requiring time and money. And the little money the guest house brought in as rent was not worth the effort and the chance to deal with people who knew their rights. The downside of leaving the guest house empty was that Barbara would need to get a job to supplement the family's income.

As time passed, it became evident to Joe and Barbara that they needed additional money to continue rebuilding the farm. Joe and Barbara understood this meant Barbara could no longer delay finding employment. It also needed to be near where Joe worked. That meant it had to be somewhere near Wolfe Road in Albany. She needed to be better equipped with her high school education being what it was, and she took a little time to examine her skills. My God, Barbara thought, I have never really developed any work-related skills. The only thing I ever do is wait on Joe and the kids. That is it, she realized, and with that, Barbara' the waitress' was born and off to Albany the next day looking for a job in a diner or restaurant.

Barbara dropped Joe off at his Hess gas station and rode down Wolfe Road looking for a job. She was surprised to find most restaurants open in the afternoon and evening. Somehow, Barbara needed to align her work hours with Joe's. Let's see, she reasoned, Joe leaves the house at four-forty-five and, being the opening manager, needs to be at work by six. That means I must leave the house with Joe at four-forty-five and be somewhere on Wolfe Road by six in the morning. The only thing going to be open at six A.M. would be a diner. That's it. There are three diners on Wolfe Road, and I need to persuade one of them to hire me.

The first stop on Wolfe Road was the largest of the three. She walked in as if she owned the place, asked for the manager, and pitched, "I have been waiting on tables for years," Barbara said, no doubt referring to serving her husband and kids. Impressed with her direct manner, the manager gave Barbara a job on the early shift, six A.M. until two P.M. five days a week. Barbara, the waitress, was not only born on that day, Barbara, now working as a waitress, was employed and going to make money starting work the following day.

Barbara was a natural. Her blonde hair and big smile were a big hit at the diner. She was polite and would laugh at all jokes presented by the customers, even the stupid ones. She quickly learned that being perfect when serving was optional and being nice to the customer was mandatory and translated to tips.

The only problem she had was that conflict with the children's schooling because she worked Monday through Friday and got up early with Joe to go to work. The school schedule was coming up shortly, and the kids needed to attend. The older two, Joe Jr. and Spring Boddy Jo, did not present a problem. They could dress and get something for breakfast themselves. Christopher, it was Christopher that would be a problem. He was now five, and experience told her he was a pain to get dressed and even harder to get fed. While she ran between customers that day, she made plans for Christopher to get to school without requiring the older children to intervene. Following her thoughts, I will dress Christopher for school before he goes to bed and make something he can take to school to eat. Barbara had laid out the plan and believed getting Christopher to school would be resolved with the older two children's help. On the first day of school, Christopher would 'hit the floor running,' so to speak.

Barbara's plan was tested on the first day of school, ten days after she created it. When Barbara and Joe returned home that day, they were greeted by the older children with "It worked, it worked." Joe Jr. said. Christopher was not a problem to get out to school; "it worked." Barbara's plan would remain in effect and replayed every school day for Christopher for the next three years. Without fail, Christopher got to school on time unless he decided to take a detour and go fishing with his other friends, as they were also ducking out of school. Christopher's skipping school came to light when he won a fishing contest during a school day, and he made the mistake of posing for a photo for the newspaper his father reviewed each day. The article read, "Young boy bags the big one!" Christopher's father bagged him later that day.

The family bills were catching up now that Joe and Barbara had jobs. The extra money put the family in a much better position and even allowed some extra cash into savings. It would not be long before Joe could afford the first item on his list and possibly the last item on Barbara's list, the tractor.

Around this time, Joe reeducated himself and learned the new trade of a 'Recovery Engineer.' Okay, many people have not heard of a Recovery Engineer. A Recovery Engineer is a person who drives around neighborhoods and picks up items sitting at the end of a driveway. That is where the Recovery part comes from. The Engineer part comes from when the recovered items picked up get converted or reused to create or fix something else: a Recovery Engineer. Should the recovered item not be usable for anything, Joe would scrap the item, giving him the new title of 'Trash Picker.' Of course, when the recovered items were too large for the Recovery Engineer to load by himself, he enlisted the untrained Barbara to do the heavy lifting, making her the 'Laborer.'

After each day's trip to work and around the local area, Joe would sort out the recovered items and pile them neatly inside the barn. He collected anything he felt could be reused and reconstructed the barn from used materials. Building something out of new materials can be a challenge. Creating something out of used junk is unbelievable!

Joe rebuilt the barn from primarily used material picked up as he traveled around the local area. The barn was restored and repainted within the first few years of living on the farm. After Joe sold the farm, the new owners allowed the barn to fall into disrepair, and today, it displays signs of being ready to collapse.

Main House and Small Garage

Large Barn as it Stands Today In Disrepair

CHAPTER TWELVE

The Tractor

I arrived at Joe's farm around eight A.M. to go on what Joe called a short road trip. Joe had already hooked up a large trailer to his pickup and was eager to get on the road to wherever we were going. "Okay, I'm here. Now, exactly, where are we going and for what?" The question I put to Joe as we slid into the pickup. "Vermont," Joe replied. "Vermont, why Vermont?" I echoed back. "Why are we going to Vermont," I said. Joe looked over at me, smiling, "To pick up my new farm tractor," then his eyes returned, looking back to driving out of the driveway.

We weren't two miles from his farm when the questions began flying around in my head. I asked Joe, "Farm tractors are thousands of dollars; where did you get that money?" I thought that was an excellent question and laid it out first. Joe's eyes left the road briefly while speaking, "Look, I got a great deal on this 'John Deere' farm tractor. I couldn't believe it when the guy called back. And I got the tractor for only two hundred bucks." For the first time, I wished I was blind, so I did not need to see this two-hundred-dollar farm tractor." Placing my left hand over my face, I remained silent and slowly moved my head from side to side. I knew little about a farm tractor, but two hundred dollars seemed meager.

The trip to the northern part of Vermont would take about two hours. I expected it to be a long and tedious ride, and it was living up to all I had imagined. Joe broke the monotony with a question, "I always wondered what happened between you and those guys threatening to burn your truck. You remember, after you closed your repair shop and needed to store the truck and a few cars in that fenced-in yard on Sixth Avenue. You remember, don't you?" "Yeah, I remember." That was my reply. "Well, will you tell me what happened or not?" Joe made a direct request for the information. I looked back at Joe and let out a loud gasp of air to begin the story he demanded to hear."

I started slowly laying out what happened in the late summer of nineteen seventy-five. Joe sat attentively upright and listened to the tale of people who were having, let us say, a misunderstanding. I began the story by saying that when I closed the shop, I did not have room at my new home for the tow truck and another car I was rebuilding. I moved them into a fenced-in lot on Sixth Avenue just south of Hoosick Street, where I thought they would be safe. About two weeks later, I received a call from 'Frenchy.' You remember him, don't you? He lived off of Sixth Avenue. Anyway, he told me Roger and the two Bender boys had some gripe with me, and they were going to burn the truck and car in the yard that night. Joe tipped his head, "Yeah, so."

I still had the Thompson Machine gun in my closet and decided to nip this problem in the bud. I grabbed the machine gun and a thirty-round clip from the wardrobe and drove to Troy to address the situation. Joe was trying hard to keep his eyes on the road and not look directly at me while I spoke but broke in with, "Well, what happened? Did you find them?" Yes, I found them sitting on the back of a red pickup truck, drinking beer and just being, as they like to say, bad. You could hear them speaking in the back of your head. "I'm bad, I'm bad, so bad" went through my mind. Well, there they were, all three of them in one place. If you remember, Roger was just over six feet tall and downright stupid. His specialty was robbing old ladies after they cashed their Welfare checks. The police arrested him repeatedly but could never prosecute him as the women were too afraid to testify. Yeah, Roger was just a nice guy, or maybe Roger was just misunderstood. The other two were brothers; I called them the Bender Boys. They were always between jobs and always had enough money for beer. And there they were, all sitting on that truck sucking down the beer and telling each other how 'bad' they were. But at least I found the three of them all in one place so I could reason with them.

I remember turning around the corner of one of the buildings in the alley, you know, of one of those abandoned buildings facing Sixth Avenue with the back to the alley, with the Thompson in my hand. And as always, for safety, pointing it at the ground. I did not want anyone to get hurt unless I had a problem explaining my position on the issues with the boys. The sun had just set, and the shadows were becoming longer in the dust of the evening. I was about forty feet from the truck when they first noticed me. It was dumb-ass Roger who was first to jump off the back of the pickup truck to confront me. As Roger approached, I lifted the gun on its side and pointed it toward him. Roger stopped briefly to focus his eyes on what I held in my hand. His following words even shocked me. "What's that you got there? Do you think you can scare me with a Fu????? toy?" It was now my turn to bring some reality to the boys. I instantly replied, "Probably not!" and I pointed the gun left of Roger at the bed of the pickup truck and shot it full of holes.

The machine gun tore straight through the truck bed, leaving holes about an inch in diameter where they entered and about three inches in diameter on their exit through the other side. The Bender boys dived down behind the truck's wheels for some protection and, as bad as they were, decided to stay there. Roger, after he heard the 'toy machine gun,' I was holding fire, lay flat on the ground, soaked in the beer he had spilled over him, pissed his pants, and was unable to speak, only mumbling something like, don't shoot. I wanted to be sure he understood me, and I approached him on the ground. Poking the barrel of the machine gun directly into Roger's face, I sent a message to my good friend Roger. To ensure we understood each other, I looked down and spoke slowly so Roger would realize the gravity of the situation. I began to tell Roger a story, "There is a man, a man with a machine gun, who just shot up your pickup truck. Do you think there is a chance he might shoot you, do you think?" If Roger could have spoken, I am sure the answer would have been yes. But I could see the yes in his eyes, so I continued, "Let me clarify myself: if anything happens to my stuff, your fault, my fault, nobody's fault, I am coming to your house. And when I get done there, it will look just like your truck, full of big holes. The only difference will be, 'You will be in it!'" I finished our man-to-man talk with, "Do you understand me?" Roger, with tears in his eyes, nodded his head quickly. He understood precisely, and my property was going to be safe. After all, Roger was betting his life on it that my property would remain safe.

Oh, by the way, here's a little side story about Roger. John Stone, the cop, pulled me over about two weeks after the run-in with Roger and the Bender boys. Do you remember John Stone? He is the officer who used to chase us down the streets on the snowmobile during the snow storms. He told me a story about someone just off of Sixth Avenue who shot a truck up with a machine gun. I look at Officer Stone before speaking, "Some crazy people here in Troy; you never know now, do you? Or do you know who that crazy person might be?" Officer Stone smiled, looking down at me, "The chief wanted me to tell you to keep that damn gun out of Troy." He continued, "Strangely, Roger has not robbed anyone since that night. All we need to do to keep Roger in line now is tell him we'll call John, and Roger breaks into sweats. But no kidding, please keep that gun out of Troy." With that, Officer Stone returned to his patrol car and left. Joe said, "Well, I am glad it was not a serious problem." Joe shook his head and smiled. Well, that's the whole story. I made my point to the boys, and everyone lived happily ever after.

The Thomson Machine

The long trip was finally ending, and shortly after finishing the story, we arrived at a rural house in Vermont. We were there, and I was ready to see this two-hundred-dollar tractor. We pulled up in front of what appeared to be a farmhouse. As we stepped out of the pickup, a large man approached, "Here for the tractor?" he spewed. "That's what we're here for," Joe responded. "Follow me out back, behind this barn building; that's where I keep it." The man said as he walked toward a large building just left where we were standing.

As we turned the corner at the rear of the large barn building, we got our first glimpse of, well, maybe, a farm tractor. The man raised his hand proudly, "Her she is, a complete nineteen-forty-six John Deere Model' A.' And with some work, it should run just like new." That was the entire sales pitch, and the man finished with a smile. I stood and tried to figure out what it would be worth in scrap iron while Joe checked the mechanicals as if he were going to take it for a ride. "I'll take it for the two hundred," said Joe. I close my eyes, thinking, take it where and how. Then I realized Brother Joe had just purchased a two-hundred-dollar coffin on wheels. But whatever it was or wasn't, we now own this two-hundred-dollar tractor.

I somehow missed the beauty in this almost forty-year-old tractor. It was as large as a small truck, with small tires on the front and tires as tall as me on the rear. The body's faded, deep green color perfectly contrasted with the rusty yellow front and back wheels. The seat, hanging on a single metal support, was made of steel, as was the steering wheel. The word 'comfort' could be found nowhere on the beast, and as far as safety equipment, well, I guess in nineteen-forty-six, you were on your own. Safety meant jumping your ass off and getting out of the way. The farmer chirps, "Yeah, they don't make them like this anymore!" And as he spoke the words, I thought: "I can see why."

The Tractor

The farmer continued, "It doesn't have a good battery, but let me show you how to start it." The two-hundred-dollars more affluent man was now offering training. The class started with, "See this lever here on the left side of the steering wheel; well, that's the throttle for the engine. This key switch right here under these three broken gages is the ignition. This stick in the middle is the gear shift, and this model has six gears. And that little pedal on the left floor is the starter push button." The man paused for an instant. "Now, I have had some problems starting it when I was sitting on the seat, so what I learned to do is get down here on the left side, open the compression release valve here, hold the carburetor lever with your left hand like this, and while leaning on this large tire reach up with your right hand and push down on the starter pedal. Oh, one thing, just be sure the tractor is in neutral, or when you push down on the starter pedal to start the tractor, it will run you over!" I stepped away from the tractor, thinking, well, that is some good information. Make sure it is in neutral, or those six-foot tires will flatten your ass right out! "The rest of it is pretty simple," he continued," put gas in the tank, and you're on your way." The training came to an end that quickly. My only thought was, "You're on your way," the man said; the question was, "On your way?" to where while images of a cemetery flickered in my head.

We loaded the beast onto the trailer using another tractor the man had in the barn building. At least the wheels turned on the loaded tractor, which might be the day's highlight. The three of us, Joe, the tractor, and I, were heading back to Joe's farm. On the return trip, Joe laid out his plans for getting this thing in 'tip-top shape' for use on the farm. As for me, I would have been happy if it had just started and could have operated safely. While sitting there on the ride back, I realized it would probably start, but as for the safety part, there was not a chance.

The two-hour trip went by without much being said by Joe or me. The only conversation was about how Joe would turn that tractor into a thing of beauty. Back at the farm, Joe glanced toward me, "What should I name it? Every tractor needs a name." I looked back at Joe and spoke lowly, "That's easy, Satan!" "No," said Joe, "a tractor is a lady; we need a lady's name." "Okay, Mrs. Satan, then." And the naming conversation ended.

The only thing left to do was unload it at Joe's farm and say goodnight. Joe now had his tractor, and I was sure the farming world would never be the same. As I drove home, I thought, let's see, a six-thousand-pound machine, you need to start by putting yourself directly in front of the rear wheel. Gages that are all broken and not functioning. The farmer did not mention the brakes, which probably didn't work. Let's get this thing fired up and go for a ride; what could go wrong?

Almost a week had passed when Joe called me again. "It runs." He said in a low voice. "Are we talking about that old tractor?" I asked. "Of course, I am talking about my tractor; what else?" was the reply. "I hope you are not calling me for an ambulance. Let me guess, you want me to come over there to see it run, right!" A brief pause followed with Joe saying, "You got it; when can you be here?"

It was after eleven A.M. when I arrived at the farm. Moving along the barn, I saw Joe and Joe Jr. in the field directly behind. As I moved forward, I could see the tractor, Mrs. Satan, near where they stood. I approached slowly, avoiding surprises hiding in the deep grass. As I came, I noticed Joe anchored the tractor to an old tree stump by a series of chains, the remains of a huge tree. "What's the game plan," was my first question, followed by Joe detailing how Mrs. Satan would 'rip the stump' right out of the ground. I stood with my mouth open before speaking, "That tractor can pull the stump right out of the ground, right?" was my question. "Of course," Joe replied. "Tractors are powerful and made to do this kind of work; step back, city boy, and let me show you how a real farmer gets things done." I tried to interject my protest, "Joe, trees have roots, and roots go in the ground deep, and I think you should dig most of it out first before you use the tractor," this was as far as Joe let me go, "Step back city-boy that stump is coming out!"

Joe assumed the position, laying against the large tire to start the tractor. I yelled, "It's not in gear, is it?" "No," Joe replied. "I got this; watch and learn." With that, I move back a little farther out of the range of Mrs. Satan. The tractor started with a pop, pop, pop, followed by other noises I could not identify. It was very slow at first but then began to pick up speed. The pops came closer together, and Joe stepped back from the tractor with a big smile. "Sounds great, doesn't it?" He spits out of his mouth. I could not answer; after all, I am just a city boy; what would I know about a forty-year-old tractor's sound? Now that Mrs. Satan was running, Joe climbed up and mounted her, you might say. After grinding some gears, Joe managed to make her move. Slowly, very slowly, the tractor moved forward, taking the slack out of the chains wrapped around the stump. I could see the tension forming in the chains, and I yelled to Joe Jr. to get away from the tractor. I now backed away, but not as slow as Joe Jr.

Mrs. Satan dug right into the dirt. The large tires began to compress, and the pulling continued. The only sound heard was the engine's now steady 'pop, pop, pop' as the tractor pulled against the stump. The tractor was now a bucking bronco; the big tires dug in and slipped only to gain traction again. Joe, or should I say 'the farmer,' held on to the wheel with both hands. Joe had set the engine throttle and locked it in place, and the only thing left was for Mrs. Satan to rip out the stump. Mrs. Satan finally achieved maximum traction, and the tires stopped slipping. The front of the tractor was now lifting off the ground, steeper and steeper. Farmer Joe could not remove his hands from the wheel to shut down the tractor as the angle was too steep. At this point, the 'safety equipment' on the tractor stepped in. That's right, farmer Joe jumped off! Mrs. Satan continued her slow climb until she came crashing down on her back. Farmer Joe, somehow uninjured, crawled over and turned off the key, stopping the popping of the engine. I paused and said, "Wow, is that how a farmer does it, Joe."

Joe Jr. said, "I told you we should have used the dynamite; that thing would have come right out and...." I stopped him mid-sentence; they needed to hear a little sanity from someone. "Dynamite, are you kidding! That stump and all of us would still be going up from the blast if you used dynamite. Shovels that is what will loosen it so the tractor can pull it out, shovels."

Joe's pickup truck flipped the tractor back on its wheels. Mrs. Satan was now able to move under her power. In just over an hour, the shovels and a saw loosen the stump from the roots, securing it into the ground, and Mrs. Satan quickly pulled it out.

As for me, I left for home still in one piece to await the next farm adventure.

Chapter Thirteen

A Farm Transformed

J oe and I were consumed over the next few years, building each of our small paradises. I was busy creating a set of small corporations in Albany, New York, and he was remodeling his farm in Pittstown. Yeah, Joe had it right. I was only a city boy, and he was the farmer making it happen with his bare hands. Joe used his bare hands to rebuild his farm, and I used my bare head to build companies. I saw it as just a different way of getting something done.

Whatever the reason, it was several years since I last visited Joe's farm. The kids were growing up very quickly, and I had not received any reports of a fatality, which I considered a good thing. It's hard to believe the kids were now in their teens and soon to become young adults. After I arrived, I sat in the car in the driveway of the farm for a moment and thought of how time was a thief that robs us every day out of something: our youth.

As I exited my car, it looked like the family was not home, even though the door to the house was open.

Someone must be here, I thought. I turned completely around, and my eyes could not believe what Joe's family had accomplished. Joe and the family had changed the entire farm. The once field behind the barn was now an oval racetrack that appeared to be almost a quarter mile in length. I noticed Joe had purchased a bulldozer, backhoe, and other equipment for the heavy-duty work the farm needed and put it to work. I did not see broken doors or missing boards on the barn, and everything looked like Joe had been working nonstop. Thinking back to the start of this farm, I realized Joe had fulfilled his dream. It looked like a farm with cows, chickens, pigs, and horses. Wait, I thought to myself. There must be twenty horses here. Why would Joe and the kids need twenty horses?

I needed to find Joe or another family member to explain why they needed all these horses. I looked around, and neither Joe nor anyone else was in sight, but what I did find further piqued my curiosity. A sulky wagon for horse racing sat in the corner of the barn, bright and shiny. I walked out to the racetrack the family built and found it covered with a soft dirt surface, recently raked. My first thought I spoke out loud, "holy shit Joe is thinking about competing with Saratoga!" I was relieved when I looked around and did not see any grandstands either built or in the process of being built. With many questions and no answers, I continued searching for my brother or another family member.

My search ended when Joe and his son appeared crossing the road where the State public lands were. "I've been looking for you guys," was my greeting. "The place looks great and much better than the last time I was here," I said. "I see you have been collecting a lot of animals and...," Joe stopped me. "I'll tell you about all that shortly, but right now, I must address a small problem with my son Joe." Joe looked at his son, "Would you like to tell Uncle John how you 'borrowed' my spare pickup truck while your mother and I went shopping? And drove it off the road on the State's land, flipped it over, caught it on fire, and it burned to the ground, or should I tell him?" Joe Jr., without a word, went into the house, which, in retrospect, was probably a good thing. Joe and I waited for the tow truck to emerge from the State lands carrying a charred body of what remained of the pickup truck. My only comment to Joe concerning the pickup was, "Probably not going to buff out!" And I left it like that. I did not say what I was thinking, but I did not believe my Brother Joe realized how much Joe Jr. was like him. I thought back to the day Joe fired the sawed-off shotgun. The pickup truck was just a bigger version of the same type of challenge, and both had the same result, 'bad shit.'

Joe had already calmed down from the pickup truck incident. He was more concerned about someone injured than the truck damaged. Besides, if Joe Jr. were going to feel pain over the pickup truck, then it would be Joe Sr. applying it.

Joe and I walked around the remodeled farm with the pickup truck event behind us. A point here and then there highlighted the new things they had done. "Looks great, Joe," I said. "It has come a long way since I last saw it, and I love your race track; what do you use it for?" Joe looked back with a smile before speaking, "The racehorse we own and train, the racehorse." I stopped dead in my tracks, "Racehorse," selecting my words to match his. Joe proudly said, "Yeah, we went out and purchased a race-horse to run at Saratoga; a pacer is what she is." How do you buy a racehorse seemed to be a good question, and that followed, "How could you afford a racehorse?" After speaking, I could not wait for the answer. My thoughts ran rampant: Has Joe managed to move up to the level of a sport reserved for kings, or had Joe brought the sport down to his level?

Joe guided me into the rear of the barn, where a tall, dark brown horse stood. Pointing as he spoke, "There she is, her name, Atagirl, our racehorse!" I knew nothing about racehorses; for all I knew, this horse could run the Kentucky Derby. It was a beautiful animal. I did not have a clue whether the horse was capable of running or pacing,

"Okay," I started. "What are all the other horses for? There must be twenty of them?" "Oh, those, we rent them for people to ride the trails around our farm and on the State of New York trails across the street." He replied. "Pays good, too." Joe finished. Finally, something that made perfect sense was renting horses for people to ride to make extra money. I looked at Joe before speaking, "Let me guess, that's the money you bought the racehorse with, right?" "You got it," Joe replied. We walked to the corner of the homemade race track. "And this is used for what exactly?" That was my opening line. "Atagirl trains here; Joey is working hard to keep her exercised and get her into shape. It won't be long before we take her to Saratoga for her first race, and we have big hopes." Joe played out the plan to me. How do you question a dream? Or, better yet, why would someone? I smiled and clarified my belief in anything he wanted to do, he could do, crazy or not.

Joe Jr. worked hard in training Atagirl, making her ready for racing. Atagirl raced at Saratoga on four occasions and, on all four occasions, finished dead last. Even as Atagirl finished last, she kept the family's dream alive. They did the near impossible by purchasing a horse, training it, and getting it into the races at Saratoga on a minimal budget. Sustaining an injury in a previous race, Atagirl ended her career at Saratoga and remains a loving memory of something they accomplished in the minds of Joe's family. For now, the sport of kings was safe, at least from Joe and the family.

The farm continued to prosper, and the children were growing up. Things were changing at an ever faster pace. It would not be long before Joe and Barbara would need to decide whether to keep expanding the farm after the children were grown or scale down for Joe's and Barbara's next phase of their lives.

The field in the photo is where Joe built the racetrack to train his racehorse Atagirl to race at Saratoga. Now overgrown and returned to nature as a grassy pasture, the track is no more. Joe's dream at the farm in Pittstown, New York, is no more, but, like all dreams, only committed to the family memories forever as a great success.

These memories will live forever in the 'We did it' realm with Joe, Barbara, and their children.

The Field where the track was built and Atagirl the racehorse trained. And now, reclaimed by Nature.

Chapter Fourteen

Leaving the Nest

A poem originally written by Leonard Lipton while studying at Cornell University in New York and later used in the song Puff the Magic Dragon by Peter, Paul, and Mary can be used to sum up the growing up of a child. The Lyrics read, "A Dragon lives forever but not so little boys. Painted wings and giant rings make way for other toys." And, of course, this also applies to little girls. As a child grows, things and values change, and other things replace them.

Spending many of Joe Jr.'s younger years on the family farms yielded many great experiences, some good and some not. There is freedom not found when living in a city. There are trails to explore while riding a motorbike or a four-wheeler and horses, with few restrictions, and you can do whatever you want. Jr. could walk out the front door directly into the wooded areas to hunt, and his father made sure he knew how to use a gun and how to use it safely. All these experiences are lost when neighbors are close, and houses line up one right next to the other. You look out every morning and view your land, the land you cultivated and maintained. A place in paradise you and your family created and where you live.

Regarding schooling, Jr. had all the opportunities of a city high school and did well in sports. Husky, that's what people said about Jr. He was Husky. Today, people would call it fat, but that is not what Jr. was. He was strong from working on the farm, producing muscle mass, and working hard, and I believe he had fun doing it. Working with your hands and learning to make something out of raw materials has been lost in our cities. Joe Jr. had many advantages, and his father made sure he learned from his successes and mistakes.

Unfortunately, as the family matures, things change, and time is the engine of all change. Children grow up and begin making their way around the world. And so, it went for Joe's children. Being the oldest of the three, Joe Jr. was much like his father. If there was a job to do, Joe Jr. was there. Like most people growing up on a farm, he was unafraid to work and get his hands dirty. And like his father, he developed an outstanding work ethic. His early careers ranged from working in Pizza Hut and working his way up to a manager, working in a warehouse, and settling down with a job at Regeneron Pharmaceuticals. Like his father, I believe he still has the first dollar he made, and also, like his father, Joe Jr. had dreams of where he wanted to go. How he would get there was a big question, but dreams are dreams, and I am not one to question them. The most important part of Joe Jr. was his loyalty and commitment, all learned from being part of a family.

His girlfriend, Claudette, had been with Joe Jr. for some time. That included the time when Joe Jr. wrecked his father's pickup truck, catching it on fire and leaving the truck a burned-out shell. Claudette's parents knew of Joe Jr.'s exploits and, like most parents, wanted the best for their little girl. They laid the law down to her. They demanded, "We never want you to see that boy again; he's trouble. Do you understand us?" I am not here to evaluate the effectiveness of that demand, but Claudette became Mrs. Joseph Thornton a few years later. Looking back, I rate demands made to one's children very low in the scheme of things.

From where I stand, I believe Jr. and Claudette have been a happy and loving couple for many years. Sitting here, I wonder if Claudette's parents ever corrected that demand or let it slide into time to be lost forever. For some reason, when people become parents, they believe mistakes they had made and then corrected are generically going to be passed on and avoided by their children. This theory may need to be revisited and rethought by someone more intelligent than me at some other time. But for now, we continue.

One thing is for sure: the apples do not fall far from the tree, and Joe Jr. followed his father. Thinking things out before you do them, my brother Joe never grasped. My brother followed the policy of doing it and seeing what happens. And like his father, Joe Jr. was following the same path. Joe Jr. is brilliant, not with book knowledge but with life experiences, a hard worker, has goals, and is committed to family. You don't need much money to succeed; you must stay focused and focus on details. Being the most highly educated person does not always pay off. We all know people who spent years in college and have trouble tying their shoes. Joe Jr. succeeded without a ton of money given to him. He worked for what he had. Joe Jr. grew up as a farmer; his father gave him the freedom to try things and learn, to try something and fail, and to learn from his mistakes, and he lived on a farm where accomplishments were king. In my opinion, the only people allowed to run for public office should be farmers who know how to get things done. No nonsense, how do we get this done attitude? Results are the key, and success expected, that defines Joe Jr.

I have often thought about what a good intelligence test would be. Well, if you were stranded on an island and needed to survive, who would you want with you? A lawyer, maybe a congressman, or a senator? A lawyer would file a lawsuit against the island, a member of Congress would write a law against being stranded, and a senator would talk about your problem and not come up with a solution. Does all of this sound familiar? No, the person you would like to have with you would be Joe Jr.

Speaking about learning from experience, at a recent Fourth of July get-together at Joe and Claudette's farm, fireworks after dark were the feature event. Somehow, the person in charge of lighting the collection of fireworks one at a time placed the packed boxes of fireworks to close. The entire fireworks collection became ignited, and everyone ran for cover. The fireworks show was short but unbelievable. Sky rockets bounced over the grass in all directions. Dixie Cannon Balls bounced over the lawn before exploding. Firecrackers, cherry bombs, and Roman candles played tag with everyone in attendance. Run Claudette, run! was the chant! How good can it get? Just what one would expect, a typical family gathering at the Thornton's. Hot dogs, salad, fried chicken, and all the guests set on fire or blown up. Luckily, nobody was injured or killed, and the event was a big success. Joe Jr. took all the credit for a good time and informed the guest how he planned the entire thing. Welcome to the life of a Thornton, either a good party or a lousy funeral, and both are always on the line when having fun.

In any event, Joe Jr. was the first child to leave the farm, and he and Claudette built a good life for themselves. They both have great jobs, own another farm, and, by all accounts, are enjoying the good life. Oh, a little note: the skills he learned from his father, Jr., and Claudette have rebuilt and remodeled their entire farm, and no, Mrs. Satan, the tractor is not there!

CHAPTER FIFTEEN

Christopher

Nothing beats the pleasure of owning your in-ground swimming pool. The deep blue waters beckon as you rest on the deck, surrounding your private fun in the sun water hole. Everything is great until the water hole needs to be repaired and becomes a money pit.

My swimming pool is one of those luxury items that is great when things are good. The pool is a large kidney shape of forty feet in length and twenty-plus feet in width, surrounded by an wide deck and flanked with grass and decorative plants. It was a beautiful sight until the day the pool liner began to leak water.

A vinyl liner inside the steel walls forming the pool contains the pool's water. The water is only slightly over three feet deep at the pool's shallow end, but the deep end is almost ten feet deep. The maximum depth required the bottom of the pool to transition from three feet to ten feet in a very short distance, making the bottom inclined very steep at about the halfway point in the pool. As you were walking past the halfway point in the swimming pool, the water would go from about your mid-waist to your neck in one downhill step.

As luck would have it, the leak occurred at the end of the summer season, and we decided to cover the pool and wait until spring to make the repairs. When spring arrived, my wife Kathy and I removed the cover from the swimming pool. To our amazement, about half of the water disappeared over the winter months to unknown places; twenty thousand gallons of beautiful blue water was missing. Kathy looked at me with that "I thought you said it was a slow leak" look. Realizing what she was thinking, I quickly said, "Thank God it was a slow leak, or all the water would have been gone!" All the water being gone would have been a blessing, as the remaining twenty thousand gallons of water looked like pea soup, green and brown, with a smell of sewerage. The only living creatures happy for the green water were the worms swimming in the soup and an occasional insect that landed for a short visit. There it was, twenty thousand gallons of thick and foul water, which we had to remove from our beautiful water hole.

A call to my brother Joe at his farm requisitioned a submersible pump. Joe and Christopher arrived to help around an hour later. The pump was lowered into the pool's deep end and connected to power through a lead. The pump soon began removing the green water and pushed it through a garden hose into a local storm drain while Kathy, Joe, and I watched. Christopher wandered around the backyard, playing with the dogs and trying to look fabulous for a fifteen-year-old teenager.

While the pump was draining the unwanted water, Kathy and I opened the box containing the newly purchased vinyl liner for the pool. Unboxing also proved a task as the new liner weighed over two hundred pounds, all folded into a box that was too small. But for only two thousand dollars, the liner company probably had to cut costs somewhere; It was apparent the box was the cost-cutting.

The long job of unfolding and stretching out the vinyl liner took over two hours. Finally, the swimming pool liner rested alongside the hole we hoped it would soon occupy. We waited patiently as the pump drained the water from the pool, but the pump stopped. The thick and green water was too heavy for the pump to pull the remaining twelve inches from the bottom of the pool. Kathy and I stood on the deck while Joe stood in the pool's shallow end, looking down into a hole over ten feet deep containing hundreds of gallons of foul-smelling sewerage, trying to devise how to remove it.

I climbed down from the deck into the shallow end. From there, I planned to use a bucket on the end of a long rope to scoop the "green water" out of the pool, one bucket at a time, handing the bucket to Joe to dump down the storm drain. As Joe and I prepared the rope and bucket, help arrived in the form of Christopher. As always, Christopher had an idea, and when Chris had an idea, everybody needed to get out of his way. But first, I decided to do it the old-fashioned way, slow but sure.

I explained my plan to Christopher, who said he would help us remove the stinking water still infesting our water hole. We all took our places. I climbed into the pool's shallow end, and Joe stood on the deck waiting to take the bucket and dump it. And the operation began, dragging the bucket attached by the rope through the green water and handing it to Joe to dump down the drain.

While we were standing in the pool's shallow end, you could see the old vinyl liner coated with dried slime. The pool liner covered with the slime was dry, but we could still feel how slippery it was under our feet. I moved cautiously, keeping my feet well-planted as I sent the bucket connected to the rope down the steep incline to gather the remaining water.

The project took a lot of time, and as most teenagers are, Christopher was impatient and offered to take over, provided he could take control of the entire project. "Let me use my idea," Chris said. "Okay, Chris," I said. "What's your plan?" Chris climbed into the shallow end of the pool. "Here's what we're going to do," he said. "I'll walk down the incline from the shallow end to the deep end, fill the bucket while you and my father pull it up with the rope, and dump it down the drain. That will make the job go quicker," Chris said with a smile. It was not for me to question Chris's plan. Chris devised an idea, and he would put it in play. Whether the idea was a good one made no difference; all I could see in my head was one of those shows you see on TV with the disclaimer, 'Don't try this at home.' You know the ones. But Chris was now in total control of the pool project, and, like his father, once they took control, I got out of their way.

Chris walked to the edge of the steep incline and placed his right foot on the downslope. "Watch this, you old men," Chris spoke with a smile. Slowly, he lifted and put his left foot on the down slope alongside his right foot. Standing still for about a second, Chris began to move his right foot for a second time. Then, Chris became a downhill skier, arms waiving to maintain his balance and moving swiftly down the slope to where a soft green pool of whatever awaited him. We were proud of how Chris kept his balance, and everything was going well until Christopher's feet struck the bottom of the incline, the flat part of the pool, where his feet stopped dead. Chris, not wanting to disappoint us, demonstrated his diving ability. He dove directly into the thick green water, face first. I looked at my brother Joe before saying, "I wonder if Chris now realizes why I did not go down the incline?" My brother Joe smiled and replied, "Maybe he figured it out!"

Chris remained at the bottom of the pool and bailed out the remaining soup. When we had finished bailing out the water from the pool, we hosed Chris off and threw away all his clothing, leaving him dressed in an old pair of jeans and a tee shirt. Chris had conquered the task of removing the pea soup from the pool and, at the same time, displayed his downhill skiing abilities.

Once again, the family came together and got a difficult job done. We laughed together with Chris and, as always, worked together as a family.

CHAPTER SIXTEEN

Spring and Walter

T hings were going well at the farm and within the
family for a long time. There were no more con-
flicts with outsiders or other issues, and Joe had finally
achieved his lifelong goal of a family and their farm.
Things were going to change, not overnight, but a change
was still on the horizon and would last years into the
future.

Spring Bobby Jo, now almost twenty, was ready to
begin her way to adulthood. Barbara got her daughter
Spring a job at the diner where she worked. And Spring,
like her mother, was a big hit with the customers. She
was slender, with blonde hair and a good personality, and
she had a steady boyfriend to help keep her in line. She
also attended college, dividing hours between school and
work. With the job at the diner, Spring made extra money
for other things, and school would secure her future.

The diner where Barbara and Spring worked as servers
was operated by Walter Hyrax Sr., who immigrated from
Poland in nineteen sixty-four. Mr. Hyra owned several

restaurants in the Upstate New York capital district area. He was famous for donating dinners every week to Veterans around the region. If anyone was down on their luck, he fed them. He never turned a hungry person away, and Walter's motto was, "Live with Passion."

Barbara was happy to work for someone who cared about people and felt that would be a good starting place for her daughter. Somewhere safe where a young girl can blossom and grow. The flexible hours meant Spring could attend the required college classes and work off times at the diner to earn extra money. Spring, like her father, had dreams, and she was well aware that achieving dreams required an education and hard work.

Spring was brilliant, and she selected accounting as her primary for college. Her eyes were focused straight ahead, her nose to the grindstone, and her mind taking in all that college could offer. Nothing could slow her down; nothing could break her focus, well, almost nothing; it was then she met Walter Hyra Jr.

Walter Jr. was a fun-loving young man about three years older than Spring. Walter Jr. worked around the family diners, filling in wherever needed. The product of a kid growing up in the late nineteen nineties more dependent on his parents than himself. By all accounts, he was friendly and fun to be around. He liked music, guns, girls, and parties and often attended places where large quantities of alcohol were served and consumed. Walter was young, handsome, from a good family, and wanted to enjoy himself and have fun. And when it came to Walter and Spring, there was chemistry. What they say about chemistry is very accurate. Spring and Walter stuck to each other like fly-to-fly paper. There was no possible escape route or exit ramp once they connected. Walter and Spring were now an 'item.'

Walter and Spring were now seeing each other daily and, within a very short time, decided to move in together. Joe offered up the spare house on the family farm, and the young couple accepted. Joe did not request rent from them. Instead, he allowed them to stay in the guest house until they could afford an apartment. The next move surprised everyone when Spring quit college, and Walter and Spring moved to New York City. The plan was to live with Walter's cousins and wait tables in the evening, and Spring would be a model. Spring was young and very pretty, but a model or modeling would require dedication and hard work. The real question was, did Spring want to go this route, and more importantly, was Walter willing to let Spring be a model? Walter was jealous of Spring, and he tried to control who she met with and who she spent time with, whether work-related or not. Whatever happened, after almost two years of living in New York City, they decided to return to her parents' farm. Once again, Walter and Spring found themselves living in the spare house belonging to Joe and Barbara, planning their next move.

Barbara's mother had lived in New Port Richey, Florida, for over twenty years. While visiting her mother, Barbara and Joe discovered the year-round warm weather. They found warm, sunny days throughout the year and no snow in Florida. Joe sat back and reflected on using the tractor, Mrs. Satan, to move the large amounts of snow that fell on the farm. After all, Upstate New York received a lot of snow every year, and living on a farm meant you maintained not only your land but, many times, the roads around your property. Some things in life are guaranteed, such as death, taxes, and snow in Upstate New York. Then, another memory flashed through Joe's head, and with all that snow came the cold, many times, very, very cold. The time to decide where Joe and Barbara wanted to live was now upon them. Do they stay in Upstate New York or transplant to Florida's warm, sunny climate? The only kid left at home was Christopher, and he was now seventeen. It would not be long before he would be out of the house. That would leave Joe and Barbara alone, with a five-acre farm to maintain, five acres that, in the winter, was covered with snow. Joe had realized the dream of the farm, and with the children now grown, it was time to move on to life without the kids underfoot. Joe looked at Barbara and softly said, "Do you think your mother can advise us on where to live in New Port Richey?" Barbara smiled before replying, "I am sure she will help us down there, but what about your job with Hess Corporation? How is that going to work out?" "I'll ask for a transfer to Florida; they are always looking for people to move down south; yeah, that's it, a simple transfer to Florida," was Joe's reply. The wheels in Joe's head began to turn, and moving to Florida was now put in motion. How and when translated in Joe's internal language, how meant, we will figure it out as we go, and when, right now.

Less than thirty days later, Joe and Barbara traveled the streets of New Port Richey, Florida, looking for a new home. Hess Corporation found Joe a new position as the manager of a Hess-owned convenience store just south of New Port Richey. The half-hour drive each way to the station was doable, leaving plenty of time to search for a new residence. The farm in Upstate New York was soon to be on the market. The only things left to do were sell the farm, pack up everything, move it all to Florida, put everything into storage until they found a new house, make the new home livable, move all the stuff into the new house, and arrange the new place to make it comfortable. Thinking back again to what his mother had always told him. "Just start at the beginning and go from there," she would say. With that thought in mind, selling the farm was the beginning, and that is where he would start.

While Joe and Barbara were down in Florida looking for a new place to live, Walter and Spring took the liberty of moving into the main house in Pittstown, New York, until the farm sold. Christopher decided to stay behind in New York until his parents could find a suitable place to live in Florida. Christopher also did not object to Spring and Walter moving into the main house and thought it best not to tell his parents. Walter and Spring decided to stay in the main house until the farm sold, however long that may take. All of this flew under Joe and Barbara's radar. Acting more like the farm owners, Walter and Spring held one hell of a party and invited everyone they knew to come over to their 'new digs,' the main farmhouse. During the party, the roads near the farm were lined with parked cars from their guests, and the alcohol flowed freely as the party raged on. The one thing that would have made Joe mad was using the home he built for his family as a party house, which was now going on in his main house on the farm. His daughter and Walter moved from the guest house to the main house, told no one, took over, and desecrated Joe's dream home with a massive party. Luckily, the property suffered only minor damages, and no one attending the party injured themselves or someone else driving home drunk.

The secret party at the farmhouse remained hidden from Joe for over twenty-three years. At Joe's seventy-fourth birthday party, he learned what happened when Spring and Walter 'watched over' his dream farm. At his party, I inadvertently let it slip out concerning the details of the party Spring and Walter held without his knowledge. Still, after over twenty years, I could see the hurt look on Joe's face of disbelief that his daughter Spring would allow a party in the dream home he had created. To Joe, it showed a total disrespect for his property and his dream. It was now apparent that Walter was making the decisions concerning the relationship with Spring, a position he felt comfortable taking and would be prominent for the next thirty years.

The farm had been placed on the market and sold in less than four months. Spring and Walter, needing a place to live, were forced to move in with Walter's mother in Watervliet, New York, and once again assessed what options were available to them. At that time, the little problems between Spring and Walter began to decay. Everyone could see the lousy chemistry, a controlling, jealous man, and a beautiful, intelligent woman. My mother would have summed it up as simply 'bad shit,' and even that definition would have fallen short of reality.

During the turmoil between Spring and Walter, she returned to college and got her accounting degree. Luck was with Spring, and she landed a job working for the New York State Attorney General's office doing forensic accounting. By any standard, this was an excellent job for Spring, and she excelled when doing it. On the other hand, Walter worked various jobs and finally landed work as a correction officer at the Albany County Jail. The job fit Walter perfectly; he was now in control at work and home. Authority is what he wanted, and that's what he demanded: total and absolute authority.

Spring and Walter purchased a house in Melrose, New York, sometime in the early 2000s. Their hard work was paying off, and life at this time held great promise. They had the promise of a family to grow and nurture, a family to enjoy life with, and a family to build a dream. The only dark cloud hanging over their life together was the alcohol and Walter's authoritarian control issues waiting to explode at any time.

The house they purchased was a single-level, light gray, single-family dwelling with green shutters and a two-car garage at the end of a long driveway. On the rear of the house stood a wooden deck for entertaining, and a sliding glass door opened into the living room area. The house sat on over two acres of land, leaving room to expand and grow. When building a family, you would want this type of home. A house that Spring and Walter could be molded into a home to meet their current and future needs. All the promises and all the dreams rested somewhere between Spring and Walter, with two small boys tagging along.

While Spring worked for New York State and Walter at the Albany County Jail, they opened a transportation business. The business consisted of moving people to and from doctors' appointments or whatever other transportation needs arose, mostly paid for by the State of New York. Walter Sr. got involved in driving for this new company, and things were going great until Walter Jr. discovered his father was allowing the less fortunate people to make a stop at a store or stop for other personal business along the way. According to family accounts, this led to a terrible argument between Walter and his father. Walter should have remembered his father's zest for life and the motto his father had set for himself, "Live with Passion." Walter Jr. clarified to his father that he was now in charge. A terrible argument ensued, and Walter Sr. quit working for the transport company. Sad as it may be, the two parted, never to speak again. Walter Sr. died in twenty-twenty-one, never having spoken to his son again. Walter Jr., after he learned of his father's passing, did what was expected of him: nothing, not even a card. Once again, he proved he was in charge.

Deep down inside, Spring knew the relationship was not going to work. Torn between happiness and pain, she was just too in love to say goodbye to the man who terrified her. During this time, Walter and Spring had two boys, Peyton and Devin. Two boys with all the promise in the world were born not into a family of dreams but instead tossed into the pits of hell.

During the next twenty years, they lived at this house, friends came less and less frequently, if at all, and Walter continued his descent into total domination of everyone around him. Things would get better and then worse without reason. The single trigger link appeared to be the alcohol, the alcohol Walter relied on, the alcohol that made him a man. The fights between Spring and Walter were common, with Spring sometimes locking herself in a bedroom for her safety. Stories from close friends speak about her staying in the bedroom away from Walter for long periods. As always, each fight was followed by an apology from Walter and the promise never to do it again, a promise that meant nothing to a dictator.

To make things even worse, Spring became ill with Lyme disease. Now unable to work, Spring found herself on disability. The symptoms of Lyme disease could include debilitating fatigue, muscle and joint pain, headaches, mental fog causing difficulty with memory or finding words, irritability, and sleeplessness. Just what Spring needed in her life, a disease limiting her defenses against Walter's aggressive nature. Trapped between a man who believed he was the ruler of the world and the debilitating Lyme disease, her life continued to crash in on her.

Walter's abuse became an almost daily event toward Spring and the children. Walter, during these drunken states, had been known to assault Spring and smash appliances and even the boy's computers in what could only be called totally out of control. The combination of Walter's alcohol problem associated with him being a corrections officer who demanded total respect could overpower even the strongest of women. One thing that came to light often was that, being a corrections officer, Walter had a gun, and Walter made it known he was willing to use it. Walter repeatedly told Spring that he knew and was ready to use his weapon, adding another level of fear to the relationship. Walter's total loss of control was becoming a daily event and threat against Spring and the children, the remnant of their lives for almost sixteen years.

The breaking point came on December 15, 2016, and continued into the early morning of December 16, 2016.

The narrative on the Intake Report read as follows: "On the night of 12/15/16, Walter (father) physically assaulted Spring (mother) in the presence of Payton (16) and Devin (11). Spring sustained a split lip from Walter, striking her in the face. Walter was out of control and destroyed the home, throwing and smashing household objects with the children in the same room. Payton attempted to intervene and hold Walter back from Spring. Devin ran out of the home and hid in the family's vehicle. Walter chased Devin outside and smashed the car he was hiding in. The children were not harmed. There is a history of Walter physically assaulting Spring and getting violent and out of control in the presence of the children. The role of

Spring is unknown." (This narrative was taken from the December 16, 2016, intake report.)

Spring received an order of protection from Walter based on this current incident, but that is not the end of Spring and Walter. Authorities had now documented the years of domestic violence in the home, and Walter would need to clean up his act, at least for a while.

Promises made and promises broken were Walter's way of maintaining control over Spring and the family. He feared arrest and kept his out-of-control moments reduced to 'almost out-of-control events.' After all, an arrest could mean he might end up placed in jail with the inmates he controlled, which is not a good place for a corrections officer to be, as one might say.

Events move slowly in the justice system, ever so slowly. The order of protection from twenty-sixteen finally came to the attention of the Albany County Sheriff, Craig Apple. The sheriff's office suspended Walter from his corrections officer job in 2019. Walter could return to work if he received and passed a mental health evaluation.

There would be no evaluation for Walter. Walter knew nothing was wrong with him, and Sheriff Apple was just out to get him. Like any reasonable person, Walter stood alone in front of the Albany County Jail, a lone picketer or, should I say, a lone protester. The domination and anger flamed by the alcohol was now moving into paranoia, and he was going to take Spring into the world where everyone was out to get them. Walter and Spring believed the F.B.I. had hacked their computers and telephones and were spying on them night and day. Home computers, as were the cell phones, were destroyed, only for the replacements to be hacked again by an unknown person working for the government. They refused to answer their front door, knowing it was someone out to get them wanting access to their home.

The transportation company they operated was long gone, leaving the only family income to Spring's disability payment. Spring and Walter could not pay the household bills with money falling short. Spring alone could no longer make the payments on the home mortgage, moving the home into foreclosure. When you would think things could not get any worse, Covid Nineteen hit the United States. That was a disaster for people worldwide, and Walter and Spring used it to their benefit. Covid Nineteen allowed them to forestall the bank from evicting them for months. At this time, Walter, Spring, and the two boys did what any family nearly financially bankrupt would do. They packed up and went to Florida for a well-deserved two-week vacation at Spring's mother and father's home in New Port Richey. Joe and Barbara are unaware of the total evil coming from New York, but evil has its way of showing its hand sooner or later. Living in Florida and being isolated from his daughter Spring and her boyfriend Walter for almost twenty years made him unaware of who Walter was. Had Joe known what Walter was doing to Spring, Walter would have dealt with the Thornton' family values' in the worst possible way. But for now, Spring and Walter were on their way for a friendly visit.

CHAPTER SEVENTEEN

The Vacation

I pulled up to my Brother Joe's house shortly before Spring and Walter arrived for their vacation. The small S.U.V. they were driving had seen its last days several years prior, and its 'borrowed time' had almost run out. The twelve-hundred-plus mile trip from New York to Florida would have taken its toll on the S.U.V., but nothing was left to take. The vehicle parked in Joe's and Barbara's driveway was a pile of dark-painted sheet metal, riding on tires with no tread left, heavily rusted fenders, and the exhaust pipe tied up with a piece of wire. As I stared at the vehicle, I wondered why two adults and two teenage boys would travel from New York to Florida in this thing. Spring always represented herself as the most intelligent person in the family. After looking at the S.U.V., they drove over twelve hundred miles that claim would be highly suspect.

I had not seen Walter since he started going out with Spring when she was about twenty. But, before me stood a man about five foot ten who appeared older than his years. I wouldn't say I like to judge people, but something was not right, whether the way he acted, moved, or spoke, something made me feel uneasy about Walter. My mother would always tell us to watch a dog's reaction to someone they do not know. If the dog shies away or growls, they sense a problem with the person. If only this once. I wished I had brought my German Shepard along to check out Walter.

Walter smiled and spoke, "Well, what do you think about this baby? Two hundred and thirty thousand miles on her and still going strong. They don't build the new ones like this anymore." I had to agree with him that they do not build cars like that anymore, and in the almost twenty years since they made that one, I could see why. To be polite, I walked around the car, looking for the high spots to praise and comment on. I was sure there must be something good I could say about this car, but as I returned to my starting point, I failed to speak a single word. The condition of this S.U.V. was ridiculous, and as far as safe, that was one thought that never entered my mind.

At that time, I realized Walter and Spring must be the bravest people in the world. Anyone who would venture out on a long trip driving in this car must be either brave or stupid! As I turned and walked towards Joe's house, I ruled out the brave, leaving, well, you know, stupid.

During this two-week-long vacation in twenty-twenty, Spring asked her father for help moving from New York to Florida. The plan was simple: Walter and Spring wanted help moving them to Florida so they could start over. There was nothing left for them in Upstate New York. Walter's corrections officer job was gone, and the bank was closing in to evict them. They reasoned out that Spring would still get her disability payment and Walter would get a job once they got here. The boys, now both in their upper teens, should be able to adapt quickly to a new life in Florida. It was strange that during the entire stay with her parents, neither Walter nor Spring tried to find a job or at least see what was available once they moved to Florida. Spring thought everything would be great, but she failed to include Walter's domination and the alcohol in the equation.

The first time Kathy and I heard about the plan was when we went to Brother Joe's home for lunch about a week later. "Let me get this straight. They want to pack up everything and come to Florida and do exactly what?" was my question. Joe lifts his head before speaking, "Walter is going to get a job doing something. Spring has the disability income, and the boys are now old enough to get a part-time job, and ..." That is where I stopped him with my take on reality, "Joe, listen, they have failed in New York; Walter was a corrections officer who lost his job, Spring suffers from the remaining effects of Lyme disease, and two teenage boys who never worked a day in their lives. Do you see a problem here, or is it me?" I ended.

Joe stopped momentarily before replying, "They have to leave; Spring says the F.B.I. had hacked their computers and telephones and was spying on them. They have to leave!" "Stop," came flowing out of my mouth. "Why would the F.B.I. be hacking into their computers and telephones? Are they part of a terrorist group or something we don't know about? Maybe they think Walter is going to kill the president or something. Joe, this doesn't make sense. What is the real reason for the move? Come on, what is the reason?" Joe looked back before responding, "I guess it is because Spring is my daughter, and I need to give her at least a chance to regain her life. That's the only reason and the only one that counts. Once I get them here, they can live in the guest house until they get a place." I said nothing more that day as Brother Joe would do what he always did: try and make it better for one of his children. Besides, what response could I present to offset Joe's reply without making me seem like a heartless bastard?

About a week later, Joe hitched up the eighteen-foot enclosed trailer to make the trip to New York. With Joe, Spring, and Walter in the pickup cab, they were on their way back to New York. The two boys were to remain at Joe's home and wait there for the return of Spring and Walter. Joe figured it would take about twenty-eight hours each way to travel. He would let Walter and Spring load the trailer with their stuff, probably another day, and of course, he would stop over to see his son Joe and the other hunting buddies. Joe, with the plan now in place, headed to New York. It's said, "The best-laid schemes of mice and men often go awry." Awry my ass, Walter got drunk and took this awry crap to a new level!

Joe arrived at Spring and Walter's home in Upstate New York a day and a half later. The trailer was unhitched and left in the driveway to be loaded by Walter and Spring. So far, it's going as planned. The first glitch occurred within five minutes of the group's arrival. Walter walked over to the deck of the house, sat down, and, while sitting in a chair, spoke, "I'm not loading shit. I don't want to leave this house; I like it here and don't want her and the kids to leave either." Joe, looking at Spring, "Okay, what's going on? You told me you wanted to go to Florida, and now this, what do you want to do?" Spring gives Walter a look that would have killed a reasonable person and starts to speak, "We are leaving here, Walter. We are going to be evicted if we don't leave. Are you coming and going to help or stay here? Your choice." Walter, the control freak, shouted back, "No, I am not going, and neither are you, so don't bother loading that trailer; nobody is leaving, nobody, do you understand me?" Spring looked at her father, "Let's load the trailer; I can't deal with this; let's load it and get out of here." As Joe and Spring began to drag the furnishings from the home and load them carefully into the trailer, Walter got up to get a cold beer. And this routine continued all day. Joe and Spring are moving things, and Walter is downing beer after beer for his part of the move, building courage by the fluid ounce.

Without Walter's help, darkness quickly fell around them. Loading the trailer was hard enough during the light of day but almost impossible in the dark. Joe looked over to where Spring was standing, "We're not going to finish and get out of her tonight. I will stay at your brother's house tonight, and tomorrow, we will finish early and get on the road without Walter." Another plan laid in place and just waiting for the mice to arrive to make it go awry!

Joe climbed into the pickup and made the fifteen-mile trip to his son Joe's house to spend the night. The night would not have been complete without a little nightcap and the typical bull session with his son. Joe finally got into bed around ten P.M., and all was good, at least for now, well, in the world of the Thornton family.

At six A.M. in the morning, Joe had already been up for a half hour. Joe Jr. and Claudette were leaving for work and pointed to the coffee hot on the stove. Joe grabbed a cup before heading back to Spring and Walter's house to finish loading and get on the road. As Joe turned into the driveway, he saw the large pile. Walter unloaded the furniture from the trailer, broke it with a hammer, and turned it into firewood. Spring, standing on the deck, red-eyed from crying all night as Walter destroyed everything, making good his threats of what he would do if she tried to leave.

Walter had made a mistake. He should have paid closer attention to the many family stories about Joe handling problems concerning his children. Joe stepped out of his truck and casually went over to where a baseball bat was lying, picked it up, and turned toward Walter to address the issue. Joe's approach was slow and calculated as he went. The first blow of the bat struck Walter's left arm, knocking him down. The storm, known as Joe, was in full force and directed at Walter, the man disrupting Joe's family. Joe slammed the bat on the pavement next to Walter's head. Walter's eyes were wide open, and fear overcame his entire body. Walter snapped back, "You hit me!" "Hit you, hit you, no, if you come anywhere near me again, it will go way beyond hitting you. I will beat you to a pulp. Get your ass up and get in that house and stay there. If you come out here again, I will finish this, which means I'll finish you. Do you understand me, or must I make you understand?" Joe ended the conversation and placed the bat on the trailer's wheel well. Walter picked himself up and entered the house, never reappearing that day. When dealing with people, you can often look into their eyes to see if they are serious. Walter saw the seriousness at a new level in Joe's eyes and chose to stay away.

Spring and her father gathered whatever they believed could be repaired and left the rest in a pile. The reload of the trailer did not take long because most of the furniture was destroyed by Walter in one of his out-of-control moments. Finally, loaded and on the road to be far away from Walter. Spring was returning to Florida with her father, and the two boys at her parent's home would finally be free. On to a new life without the daily anger brought forth by Walter. Everything is looking up with a new future in Florida for Spring and the kids.

It was hours into the return trip that Joe learned from his daughter that Walter had thrown gasoline on Spring during the night and threatened to light her on fire if she left. Joe sat shaking his head; if Spring's father had been aware of that happening when he was beating Walter with the bat, Joe would have needed a backhoe to place Walter into his final resting place on the property. Joe looks Spring directly in the eyes before speaking, "Walter can not come to Florida. Do you hear me? No Walter in Florida." It was clear to Joe that Spring and Walter could never be a family again. Throwing gasoline on someone and threatening to light them on fire is well beyond just being mad. Mad hell, insane is the correct definition.

Collage of the Home Walter Destroyed

CHAPTER EIGHTEEN

Back In Florida

With the trip from New York to Florida behind them, Joe and Spring arrived two days later at Joe's home in Florida. Walter, now the sole member of the family remaining back in New York, was not missed. On the return trip to Florida, Joe repeatedly made Spring aware that Walter could not come anywhere near Florida or there would be serious trouble. Spring agrees and promises to let Walter stay in New York, which ends the conversation between Spring and her father. Joe, deep within, questioned Spring's sincerity, but she was his daughter; his family and family needed to trust one another.

About three weeks later, I met Spring at Brother Joe's house. The chance meeting occurred in the back patio area just outside the guest house, and my first look at Spring revealed how Walter had affected her. No longer the young, pretty blonde girl I had known. No longer the big smile and warm welcome. Her movements were quick and jerky as she spoke, and her sentences were far shorter than one would expect from a highly educated person. A cigarette always seemed to be in her hand, and her body trembled, making the smoke shake as she exhaled. What remained was the shell of a beautiful woman beaten into submission by a controlling dictator, Walter.

At this meeting, she echoed the claims that the F.B.I. hacked all their electronic devices and knew every move they made. According to Spring, this was one reason for leaving New York. I listened for a brief time and responded, "Okay, Spring. You know that I am a computer system specialist. So where are these computers and phones the F.B.I. have hacked? Let me see them." Spring's eyes moved side to side as if looking for something lurking out of sight before speaking. "We destroyed them so they could not track us! But, I have the proof, paperwork showing the hacks and proving they were listening to us." My expression cast doubt on her claims, and I followed up with, "Okay, go get the paperwork; let me see the secret surveillance hacks by the F.B.I., come on, right now!"

Spring returned holding a pile of printouts containing computer system file names. As she handed them to me, she spoke, "There they are, proof they hacked us and were watching what we were doing." I started to review the filenames on the printouts, which revealed something far different than the claims made by Spring. "Spring, from what I see here, these are a collection of trackers used for advertisers. See here; this file is considered malware and directs you to websites for ads. This one tracks the number of times you visit sites, and here ...." That is when she stopped me and said sharply, "You're in on it; you work for the F.B.I., I knew it; you're one of them, watching me and watching Walter!"

I started slowly, "Listen, Spring, If the F.B.I. wanted to spy on you, you would not know it. Who told you about all of this F.B.I. spying and other crap?" She nodded, "Walter, Walter told me. He was a C.O. and had connections with law enforcement. A friend told him they were watching, watching, I tell you, watching! That's why we don't answer the phones and use the computers; they listen to everything, trying to get something on us." I now realized what had happened; what Walter had done was evident to anyone stepping back and looking from the outside. Walter found another way of taking complete control of Spring by isolating her from everyone. Leaving only Walter as her support person, and she could not trust anyone because if they did not go along with the hoax, they must be a secret agent of the government. Unfortunately, convincing Spring of this hoax was impossible until she had time away from Walter. Spring needed time to break the bond and fear he instilled in searching for the boogeyman. Walter had created a mythical world for Spring where only he and he alone were there to protect her. Everyone outside that world worked for the government and was a spy watching every move Spring and Walter made, trying to catch them doing illegal things, whatever they might be.

Spring, now living in Joe's and Barbara's guest house in Florida, started working on her financial problems. She figured out how much they could afford for rent and other necessities so she and the two boys could move into a new place. A month passed, and then a second month was gone before she accumulated enough money to make their move. One problem remained. To my surprise, the old S.U.V. had died. The surprise for me was that it continued to run as long as it did. But now she needed a car to move around Florida. Spring approached her father and convinced him to co-sign a loan for a new car. Two days later, Spring purchased a new K.I.A. with the help of her father's signature. Spring found a house to rent south of New Port Richey a week later. She could afford the rent and the car payment, and true to form, her father moved all their possessions into the newly rented house. Spring assured her father she would not tell Walter where they had moved, and she would never see Walter again. After hearing the story of the events in New York, I believe Spring's not seeing Walter was the best for all involved. I knew that if Walter came to Florida, my Brother Joe would complete his family obligation of 'lighting him up' to defend Spring.

Less than three weeks after they moved into the newly rented house, Walter arrives from New York and moves in. Joe and Barbara were unaware of Walter's arrival or that he moved back in with Spring. All the claims made by Spring about Walter not knowing the address and could never find her were bullshit. When her parents learned Walter was living in Florida with her, she defended the broken promise by saying, "The boys wanted their father here with them." Spring broke her repeated promise to her father concerning Walter's return to live with her. Spring now could return to the world where Walter was king, and her duty in life was to listen and obey. Anyone looking at the chain of events would have seen the danger lurking in the dark, anyone but Spring. Dictator Walter told Spring what she wanted to hear, that he had seen the light and changed. The only thing that changed was the location of the abuse. All that Walter needed now was some alcohol to lubricate his ego and place him back on top in total control.

Barbara would sometimes travel from her home in New Port Richey to the house where Spring lived to spend some time with her daughter. Although Spring's car sat in front of the house and Barbara could hear voices from inside, no one would answer the doorbell. The pattern of not answering the front door had now moved from New York to Florida. Playing not home was a way to avoid the surveillance of Spring and Walter's family by government spies. The people walking down the street were watching them. The F.B.I. staffed a trash truck trying to get a view of them. The telephone would ring, not to be answered by Spring, Walter, or the children. The door knocks went unanswered. Walter had again convinced Spring the Boogeyman was after them while they hid locked between the four walls of their fortress or prison without bars.

For the next eight months, things appeared to have calmed down between Spring and Walter, and during this time, Peyton, the eldest boy, left and moved to Fort Myers. Peyton landed a job as a car salesman and started doing well enough to rent a small apartment in Fort

Myers. Also, during this time, Joe and Barbara stayed away from where Spring and Walter were living, except for the trips Barbara made alone to see her daughter, which usually failed. One thing was clear: Walter was not allowed near Joe's and Barbara's home. Was this a perfect arrangement? No, but it was better than the alternative. Walter could not bother Joe, and Joe could not get his hands on Walter. Joe remembered Walter throwing gasoline on Spring, and Joe planned to 'light up Walter,' literally, for doing it if he got his hands on him.

True to form, Walter took control and pressured Spring to stop paying the house rent. He tried to claim a Covid Nineteen exemption for not paying the rent. Of course, this led to the landlord filing for an eviction. A week later, the eviction notice was served to Spring by the Sheriff's Department, demanding their immediate removal from the rented house. With nowhere to go and little money, Spring contacted her son Peyton to see if they could move to Fort Myers and start over living in his small apartment. Peyton agreed to let them move into his small apartment in Fort Myers. There was only one problem. They had no way to move anything, anywhere. Their only transportation was the K.I.A. car, which made them unable to move much of anything. Spring did what she always did: calling her father to help her move to Fort Myers.

"No, not with Walter there! I am not going there with Walter! He's a piece of shit, Spring, why can't you understand that?" was Joe's answer to his daughter during the call for help. "He threatened to light you on fire, remember! What is wrong with you? How often have you told everyone how smart you are and are still living with that idiot? Please." Joe paused, waiting for an answer. There was a pause before Spring answered. "No, Walter won't be at the house; he will go away until we finished; he won't be here," was the reply. Joe sat back in his chair before speaking, "I will bring the trailer, and you and your son will help load it. And everything must be outside on the sidewalk and ready to load before I arrive. I don't want anything to do with that bastard Walter. When we get to Fort Myers, we will unload the trailer and put the stuff on the sidewalk outside the apartment. You and the boys can put it in the apartment. And remember, No Walter around me! That's the deal, take it or leave it." The deal was sealed with Spring saying, "That will be good enough," and hanging up the phone.

Joe was unhappy with what Spring had done concerning Walter's coming to Florida and poured himself another afternoon beverage. He sat on his patio and tried to understand why she would do something that stupid. He closed his eyes, and thoughts streamed through his head: she was a college graduate. What is she thinking? But as always, he would try to help his daughter and do whatever it took for her. Being a good father, Joe was too close to see Spring and Walter's life together as a balancing act of love and hate. The love made things good, and the hate added excitement, as crazy as that may seem.

The following day, Joe and Barbara hitched up the eighteen-foot enclosed trailer before heading to the house Spring had rented only months before. Upon arrival, Joe noticed the K.I.A. car Spring had purchased was missing. He assumed Walter must have taken it somewhere to avoid meeting with Joe as requested and agreed to by Spring. Also, the furniture and boxes were being moved from the house and placed on the sidewalk. Spring and her son continued to pack and move the household things one box at a time for the next hour and a half. Finally, they finished packing; the house was empty, packed, and loaded into the trailer, preparing for the trip to Fort Myers.

"That's all of it," Spring yelled. "Great," Joe replies. Barbara says, "Before we leave, we should use the bathroom; after all, it's a two-hour trip to Fort Myers from here." As she locks the door, Spring suggests, "Why don't we wait and go down to the convenience store on the corner, get gas, a soda, or something..." Joe says, "No, I don't want to stop so close to here. Let's use the bathroom in the house and get on the road."

Grabbing the key out of Spring's hand, Joe unlocks the door and steps into the house, with Barbara following close behind. Entering the home, they find significant destruction. Walls had holes punched through, power outlets smashed, and damage everywhere. As Joe stood at the bathroom door, he saw the toilet broken and the sink badly damaged. Yeah, Walter, Walter was right back to his old tricks. If he can't have it, nobody will have it. Joe stands outside a moment before asking Spring, "What happened here? Joe acted as if the answer could be anything other than Walter's damaged the house. "

Spring turns away, "Well, Walter got mad when they filed for the eviction. You know how he is about that kind of stuff. He just got mad and broke some stuff. But he promised to get better!" was Spring's reply. Joe could only turn and walk away after an answer like that from Spring; it seemed now confirmed his daughter Spring was either stupid or brain-damaged from the beatings by Walter. Without options to help his daughter, Joe relented and realized he was her father and not her savior on that day.

The house relocked, and they climbed into the truck for the two-hour trip. Few words were to be spoken by either Joe or Spring as they drove to Fort Myers. The two-hour journey dragged on for what seemed to be forever. After all, what could be said? If Spring did not know by now, the devil she was living with, no one could help her. Joe sat silently driving down the highway to Fort Myers, remembering his little girl, now a woman but still as afraid of the dark as when she was ten, and not realizing Walter was the source of those fears.

The truck pulled to the curb as they arrived in Fort Myers just before three P.M. As agreed, Joe unloaded the trailer and placed the items on the sidewalk. Spring and her son were taking the items and moving them into the apartment. Once Joe had the trailer unloaded and emptied, he closed the doors. As they had agreed, the move to Fort Myers was complete.

The departure was, at best, a cold goodbye. Joe and Barbara waved and continued saying goodbye as they left, but you could cut the tension with a knife. It would be best if you cut your losses, and Joe and Barbara have finally reached that point, at least for now.

On the long return trip to New Port Richey, the atmosphere was like a funeral; Joe mentioned the K.I.A. car he helped Spring purchase. "Spring said she needed the car to get a job here in Florida. As far as I know, she has never applied for a job. I guess she fooled me again." Finally, Brother Joe realizes that Spring is not honest with him. Whether he would accept it, the jury was still out.

CHAPTER NINETEEN

Return from Fort Myers

F our months have passed without hearing from Spring, who decided to live in Fort Myers with the idiot Walter. Four months without a single word about anything. No Spring, no Walter, no problems, four months of peace at Joe's home in New Port Richey. Joe and Barbara returned to their retired life of making lawn ornaments, doing outside maintenance, and spending afternoons on the patio watching television. Joe believed Spring was finally on her own in Florida to make whatever way she desired. Finally, free from the craziness his daughter brought to his door, he was free. Well, free; the question was free for how long.

I was sitting on Joe's patio when the telephone rang. "Hello, what's wrong? Call me later." Joe's conversation with the unknown person on the phone ended abruptly. "Who was that?" Joe replied, "I don't know what is wrong, but it was Spring on the phone, and she said she could not talk right now. I think she was crying." Joe replied. I could feel my blood pressure rising with that answer. Kathy and

I had long ago figured out Spring was terrible news for the family. I knew it was going to be bullshit, whatever it was, and I did not want to sit there too long and tell Joe what I thought. "Well, I need to go home right now to help Kathy; call me when you find out. You know it has to be asshole Walter, don't you?" Was my comment as I walked down the paved walkway, exiting the patio area.

Early afternoon the following day, I heard from my Brother Joe. Spring had called him back and described what had happened for the last few months while living in Fort Myers. "Don't tell me on the phone; I'll come over." I thought to myself, this has to be good. Four months, and now she calls. "Joe, I'll be there in twenty minutes." I hung up the phone, and Kathy and I got into my car. On the trip over, I envisioned the brawls that must have occurred between her and Walter. Yeah, some downright dragged-out fistfights. I wondered if her older son got involved. Did they toss Walter out on the street, or maybe Walter tossed them out on the street? Whatever it was, it had to be unbelievable when it came to Spring and Walter. And I was ready for anything, well, almost anything!

Kathy and I arrived at Joe's house within a half hour of the phone call he had made to me. I sat in a chair on the patio before speaking, "All right, what's the story now? Who hit who?" I asked. Joe sat back, holding a drink he usually reserved for later in the day. "She needs to come back here, her and her son Devin. The lease in the apartment is ending, and she has nowhere to go." I shot back, "What about Walter?" "Spring said he is staying in Fort Myers, and she wants to come here," Joe replied. I took a moment to gather my thoughts. "You mean to tell me she did not know when you moved them to Fort Myers that the lease was ending in a few months? Is that what you are trying to tell me?" Spoken with total disbelief. Joe, looking away, mumbled, "I think that's the story." You're not telling me the whole story. I will sit here and not say a word while you tell the entire story. "What is the whole story," I asked and sat back to listen. As I turned, I could see Kathy on my left, shaking her head from side to side and closing her eyes. I could tell by the expression on Kathy's face she was saying to herself, 'This has to be good!'

Joe started at the beginning, "When she made a deal with her son Peyton to move and live in Fort Myers, he had only four months left in his lease. Peyton met a girl and moved into her apartment over a month ago. Spring tried to renew the lease in her name, but the landlord of the house they rented near New Port Richey is trying to sue her for Walter's damage to the house. Oh, and in November, she had Walter locked up for beating her up, and now he is out of jail. He agreed to stay in Fort Myers when she came back here. And ... "Stop, have you lost your damn mind?" I injected into the conversation. Continuing, "You moved them from New York to Florida, you helped her purchase a car so she could get a job, you moved her to a new apartment, she brings Walter down from New York, Walter destroys the rented apartment, you move them to Fort Myers, and now Spring wants to come back here, are you for real, better yet what about the job she was going to get, it has been almost two years, what about the job?" Joe did not answer momentarily and looked up slowly, "She is my daughter; I need to give her a chance. I know it sounds stupid, but..." I rose to my feet before speaking, "No, Joe, stupid is when you make a mistake once without all the needed information. Joe, this is beyond stupid; it borders on the definition of crazy, which is doing the same things repeatedly, expecting a different outcome; crazy, that is what this is. But it is your decision, and Kathy and I will support it; think crazy for a while as you sit there and make sure it is what you want to do. Oh, one last thing: I don't believe she is telling you the entire story, and Walter will be here sooner or later!" Kathy and I got up from our chairs and walked down the path, leaving the patio area. We slid into our car, leaving in a fog of total disbelief. Just staring out the car's front window, Kathy and I began the drive to return home. Kathy and I talked about what we had just heard and agreed that Walter would return to New Port Richey sooner or later. Spring had lied about everything since she moved to Florida, and I could see nothing that would make her change.

On February 1, 2023, Joe and Barbara traveled to Fort Myers to move Spring and Devin back to New Port Richey. There seemed to be much less to load and bring back, and I assumed Walter had destroyed everything else. But here she was, back again, Spring and her son living in Joe's guest house. As for myself, I made myself scarce and visited Joe's house less frequently. There was no secret that I believed Spring and Walter were nothing but trouble, and an argument over there would not help anything.

When Joe and Barbara stopped at my home, sometimes parts of conversations with Spring would slip out. At one point, during an argument with her mother, Spring blurted out, "If I told Walter to shoot you, he would!" During another outburst, she slapped Barbara in the face. As I listened to this, I shook my head, "She has to go; look, Spring needs to go; this is not good for any of you," is all I could say. My words fell on deaf ears, and Barbara was convinced Spring in time would change for the better. I, on the other hand, believed that, in time, things would only get worse.

Spring started taking her dog for three-hour walks sometime in April. She would put the dog into the car and disappear for hours. Kathy and I questioned this immediately, "Joe, we think Walter is back here somewhere." Barbara would always answer, "No, Spring just told me Walter is in Fort Myers; he has a car and a room and delivers food for money to support himself; he is not here; she told me so." Kathy and I both knew Joe and Barbara were lying to themselves, only hearing what they wanted to hear from their daughter. I remember something our mother told me years ago, 'you can lie to your banker, you can lie to your boss, but never lie to yourself.' My mother was right: once you start lying to yourself, you become part of the problem.

The next strange occurrence with Spring was about six weeks later, sometime in June, if memory serves me correctly. Spring's car was not in the driveway all night, every night! Barbara was the first person to question Spring where her car was every night. Spring's answer was as follows: "Well, you see, Walter had to leave where he was staying in Fort Myers. He had a rental car but lost that, and now he is staying in New Port Richey. he can't come here, so he is sleeping in my car in the Lowes parking lot, and after I get up, I go and pick him up and get the car in the morning."

Now, there was no question Walter was back and close in New Port Richey. All the promises made by Spring were once again all bullshit. The promise that she was not in contact with Walter lies. The promise Walter was staying in Fort Myers lies. The commitment that she would have nothing to do with Walter lies. All lies, lies! My question was, what is Spring not telling them? This entire chain of events smelled like week-old fish in a sink, and I knew Spring was trying to cover up their stink.

Joe did not handle the information about Walter's return very well. He had co-signed the loan on Spring's car, and now Walter, the man he hated and abused his daughter, was using it as a night residence and probably to make food deliveries to make money. "Walter is not using that car to sleep in," Joe yelled. "I don't care where he sleeps or lives, but not around me. Do you understand me, Spring, not around me, and if you can't fix this, you should leave too. Let Walter take care of you. I've had it, had it, do you understand!" Ending Joe's ranting, and he walked away. Spring now had a big problem; she allowed Walter to return and tipped her life upside down again.

Spring, now caught in all the lies she pushed out to her mother and father, needed to fix things quickly.

Spring's youngest son, Devin, had turned seventeen and had just applied for a driver's license. Spring and Devin purchased a used car for about twenty-five hundred dollars at a local dealer. After seeing this car, junk would be a good description. Bald tires on a rat sedan on wheels are how I would describe it. A cheap minimum insurance policy and plates gave Walter a car to deliver food for money and sleep in. The problem was fixed, well, according to Spring.

The stage for a looming disaster was complete with Walter close to the family, and all his hate and anger were stored deep. Walter knew others caused all of his problems. He did not know who was causing them, but he knew it was someone. And that made no difference. Anyone within his reach would do, and Spring brought him back close to her family well within his reach.

To sum up the situation. A person with apparent mental issues, living in a junk car in a Lowes parking lot, likes to drink large amounts of alcohol, get drunk, and be close to the people he hates. My mother had it right, this was "Really Bad Shit!"

This series of events is beyond stupid and borders on a plan, but a strategy to do what was the question. Why would a person whom Walter had abused for years bring him to where she and her family lived? Was Spring stupid or just afraid?

One could almost hear the minutes, hours, days, and weeks past as with the clock ticking, waiting for Walter's next out-of-control event. Deep within the silence, as consistent as a heartbeat, the steady, Tick, tick, tick!

And then came a disaster, Hurricane Idalia screaming in from the Gulf of Mexico!

CHAPTER TWENTY

Idalia & Murder

As the west coast of Florida readied for Hurricane Idalia to make landfall, Walter and Spring attended a small party in New Port Richey, Florida. Walter had reconnected with two old friends he knew when he lived in the Albany, New York area, and they decided to celebrate the hurricane with a small party. Walter was well on his way to being drunk when he arrived, and the party further gave him permission or a reason to continue drinking.

It did not take long for the problems to begin, with the anger stored deep in Walter beginning to vent and directed toward Spring. The verbal abuse turned physical with the addition of aiming a gun at her head and threatening to kill her and her entire family. Walter demanded Spring and himself get back together and continue their excellent relationship while holding Spring by the throat. The homeowners intervened long enough for Spring to break free of Walter's grip and make an escape to her car. Spring, now out of the house, drove the three-mile trip back to her parent's home for safety. Walter remained at the party alone with the homeowners and, of course, the alcohol and the gun. Walter was still drinking heavily, and with the alcohol running out, the homeowners made a decision. The partiers purchased another eighteen-pack of beer, and Walter finished it off quickly. Not long after drinking the newly purchased beer, the problems with Walter returned, this time directed at the homeowners. The gun made another appearance, followed by more threats and erratic physical motions again directed at the homeowners. The homeowners demanded Walter to leave the home. Walter complied, staggered out, and got into his car, voicing threats as he went. At least for now, Walter's 'Old Friends' felt safe from Walter. Unfortunately, what happened was the release of a drunken, crazed man looking for the people who ruined his life, Spring's family! As Walter drove away, the homeowners did nothing to protect the public from Walter driving drunk and armed with a pistol he used to threaten people. They did not call for police assistance for the man they allowed to become drunk and out of control, nothing. The only thing the homeowners did was pick up the telephone and call Spring to warn her that Walter was gone and uncontrollable.

The telephone rang just after ten P.M., finding Spring awake in her parent's guest house. Picking up the phone, "Hello," Spring answered sharply. The voice on the other end of the line babbled, "Walter just left here, and we don't know where he is going; he may be heading towards you. He's drunk and mad as hell, and he still has the gun;

watch out, he has the gun!" The call ended with those final words.

Spring sat back and continued to smoke her cigarette. What now, she thought. It all seemed like a rerun of what happened in Fort Myers in November 2022, months before. She was now placed into a box as she had not told her parents about everything in Fort Myers. There was no mention of Walter's out-of-control moments leading to him being arrested and jailed. There was no mention of Spring refusing to press charges, which led to Walter's release. And there was no mention of Walter possessing a gun. Once again, she only told her parents enough to force them to help her out of a situation she had created alone. Spring closed her eyes, reviewing the November events, and the images came rushing back. It was then Walter threatened her with a gun, it was then she found the courage to call the police, it was then Walter was arrested and jailed for making threats with a weapon, and it was then she refused to continue pressing the charges, which led to his release. She stepped outside, stared into the darkness, closed her eyes, and thought, what do I do now?

The police booking record for November 21, 2022, was as follows:

Person	
Name	HYRA, WALTER JR.
Number	366237
DOB	11/7/1972 US
Race	W
Sex	M
Height	5'10"
Weight	210lbs
Address	5591 SPECTRA CIR FORT MYERS FL 33906
Booking	
Number	960153
Booked On	11/21/2022, 5:36:00 AM
Housing	
Status	Released
Released On	12/13/2022, 10:32:00 PM

The charge: Aggravated Assault with a deadly weapon without intent to kill

Well, she thought, the police did not believe he was going to kill anyone when he had the gun pointing at her. She recalled reading that in the police booking report. His way of blowing off steam went streaking through her head. That is what it is, just blowing off steam. She kept repeating this as if that would make it something a reasonable person would do. Spring turned and re-entered the guest house and slowly walked over to the bed. It was then she heard the door slowly open. "I'm here, Spring," said a drunken voice in the night behind her. "Walter," Spring whispered as she turned around. Spring's memories of the events from Fort Myers ended abruptly. There stood Walter, drunk, anger in his eyes, and holding the gun in his right hand. Walter approached and pushed Spring down on the guest house bed and tried to force himself upon her. Spring struggled and got him off of her and moved away.

Spring, in her most forceful voice, "You're not supposed to be here; my parents don't want you here; get out of here, you idiot!" Walter lifted himself off the bed, "I want to be with you, and your family is keeping us apart," he spoke as if those were words of love. All while smashing the television with the pistol in his right hand. "I belong with you, and you belong with me," followed, destroying whatever things he could reach within the small room. Spring moved through the door leading to the outside of the guest house, and Walter followed. Reaching the outside, she stepped off the small porch and moved to the center of the patio. Walter followed again, destroying everything as he went. The large outside television, stereo system, and glass table all fell victim to Walter. "Your family is keeping us apart, your family," Walter's slurred voice echoed. With that, Walter turned and headed up the single path to the main house. Spring stood without a scream, without getting to her phone to call the police, nothing, just stood there and lit another cigarette.

View of the Path from the Guest House to the Main House

There is only one path between the guest house and the main house; once on this path, Walter can only go to the main house. Walter traveled the fifty-foot path leading directly to the stairs, staggered up the five steps onto the home's rear deck, and quietly opened the sliding glass door into the kitchen. Spring's mother and father lay sleeping in their bedroom while Walter moved through the kitchen. Drunk with alcohol and anger, Walter moved toward the bedroom door to make a settlement with the people keeping him away from the woman he loved.

Joe did not know for sure what woke him from his sleep. The squeak of the bedroom door hinges, the door handle's click as it turned to open the door, or maybe a flicker of light from the kitchen that should not have been there. Joe did not know for sure, but as he awoke, he made out the image of Walter, Walter standing in the bedroom door, Walter with a gun mumbling, "I'm going to kill you and your bitch wife right now. Cloudy-eyed and half-asleep, Joe jumped and lunged at Walter. Two shots were fired and absorbed by Joe's left shoulder in his effort to subdue Walter. Joe instinctively wrapped his right arm around Walter's neck, and they fell onto the bed where his wife was lying. The gun spoke again, blowing a hole through a closet door, and repeated the same short outburst, destroying a long mirror. As the struggle continued, Joe pushed his wife Barbara onto the floor using his right leg to put her out of the line of fire. Another loud burst from the gun punched a hole into a wall, followed by the weapon pressed against the right side of Joe's head, where the gun made its final report.

Walter was now free from Joe's grasp and moved out of the bedroom into the kitchen. The six-shot pistol was, for the moment, unusable, and Walter, in his drunken state, searched his pockets for more bullets, the words used to make the gun speak, to reload again and finish his task. Unable to find the words in his pockets, Walter gazed into the darkness of the kitchen, looking for something else, anything lethal, to finish the deed. The last thing Walter expected was to see the person he had just shot in the head grab a large knife from the kitchen counter and move toward him to attack.

The gun, worthless and now unable to speak, would be no match against the person he believed he had just killed, wheeling a large knife. Walter fled through the unlocked garage door to the outside of the home. Exiting the house, he jumped into the car he had left in the driveway and escaped. Joe stood, badly wounded, by the open door, holding the knife over his head, and waited. He waited for Walter to return, probably with another fresh load of bullets to finish the job he had started.

Joe's wait ended when he finally collapsed and drifted into unconsciousness, laying in a large pool of blood on the kitchen floor. The badly wounded body of Joe did not witness the screams of terror from his wife Barbara as she called 911. Joe did not see his daughter wrapping his head in towels, trying to stop the bleeding. Joe was not aware of the EMT's arrival or his transportation to the local trauma center. No, Joe was not aware of the dozens of officers starting the homicide investigation at his home. Joe was not aware that he may well be a victim of a murder! Joe lay unconscious, fighting for his very life after successfully defending his family from an attacker determined to kill both his wife, Barbara, and himself.

No one was aware of the fate of Walter, who was less than five miles away and now cornered by the police. In his last act of desperation, once again, the gun, reloaded with the words found in the glove box, spoke. This time, the victim was Walter himself, attempting to take his own life with a single shot to the head. The anger finally released, and his night of terror ended on a lonely street in New Port Richey, Florida. He died just as he had lived, alone and afraid, haunted by the demons from within.

CHAPTER TWENTY-ONE

A Sad Story

As Hurricane Idalia came ashore, the winds and rains intensified. It could not be exceptionally comforting for anyone who has not experienced a hurricane. The winds and rain increase quickly; within minutes, it is almost like magic seems to stop. The weather forecasters call this the 'band effect of the storm,' I call it unsettling. Kathy and I were glued to the television, watching the Weather Channel for the latest update on how we would be washed away into the Gulf. With all emergency items, we waited for the storm of the century to fall upon us. The hurricane we expected, the following events we did not.

The telephone rang just after eleven P.M. in the evening, and Kathy answered. A stressed voice on the other end of the line gave way to the message going to be delivered. Speaking softly and ever so slowly, "It's Joe, Joe's been shot. Walter shot Joe; he is at Bayonet Point Trauma Center. Come quickly." The call ended without a reply.

Kathy and I found ourselves traveling south to Bayonet Point Hospital as the bands of Hurricane Idalia moved onto the shore of West Florida. The road called U.S. Highway Nineteen was beginning to flood. The winds were rocking our SUV, and the rain sometimes blinded almost total view of the highway. The trip of about ten miles took nearly a half hour, and the only break we caught occurred as we parked the car, and the rain stopped long enough for us to hurry into the building.

As we entered through the doors marked trauma center, Jamie, our niece, greeted us. "He got shot in the head," Jamie said. The words put forth gave images of a total disaster. "Is he alive?" Kathy replied. "We don't have an update yet; he has been in there for a while; we don't know how bad he is." Jamie's response boarded on hysteria as she spoke. I cut in, "Okay, let's get together and wait for the doctors to give us an update. Where is the rest of the family." She pointed to a room around the corner from where we were standing.

As we turned the corner, Barbara sat staring straight ahead. After a brief discussion with her, I realized she only remembered a little about the events of that evening. Barbara could only recall calling the police, who were all around the house when she left. It was evident none of the family members there had news, good or bad, and the wait for the doctors began.

The wait for the doctor's verdict took about an hour. Four doctors walked in from the secure trauma area and approached us. Stoned-faced, they came, and I braced for the worst. The lead doctor began, "Well, he is stable.

It looks like the bullet traveled out and not in. Additional scans will verify that, of course. He has been placed into a coma to avoid more damage. But he is alive and very fortunate." Shot in the head and still alive was about all the good news we were going to get that night. Tomorrow was going to be the decision day, and with nothing else we could do that night, I suggested we go home and return early in the morning.

Sleep that night failed to come for any of us. I kept reviewing our warnings to Joe and Barbara concerning Walter and Spring. Joe was so worried about doing what was 'right' for his daughter that he put Barbara and himself in danger. There was no mention of Walter that night by anyone present. None of us knew Walter's fate, whether he got away or captured. It did not make any difference. Without Spring, Walter had no power, and I knew where Spring was, still in the guest house at Joe's home.

I found the entire family at the Bayonet Point Hospital the following day. The waiting area was almost void of non-family members as we waited for a more definitive word concerning Joe's injuries. Barbara sat in a corner, staring into space, and could remember little, if anything, of what had occurred only hours before. As I circulated among the family, I made it clear not to speculate about how Joe was or the extent of his injuries. We needed to wait and hear from the doctors directly about his condition, and guesses and rumors were not going to make Joe better.

As the wait continued, a female officer approached, seeking information about the previous night's events. The questions she proposed to Barbara yielded nothing and possibly even more confusion to her report. I pulled the officer off to the side and related a fact she should now be aware of: Barbara had blocked all the details concerning the entire event. She nodded in agreement and started to turn and leave. I asked as she turned, "Oh, did they catch Walter?" She stopped looking puzzled before replying, "Nobody told you; Walter shot himself in the head and is brain dead on life support." I paused before replying, "No, no one told us anything about Walter; he is brain-dead," I repeated. "Yes, the report says no detectable brain activity." She replied. One might think my next thought would make me a terrible person, "good, that bastard is dead!"

I called the adults over to one side of the room and related the 'good' news given to me by the officer. "Walter was brain dead by his hand" were the words I used. No one in attendance showed remorse for Walter's passing or at least near passing. Brain dead or no brain activity, whatever, close enough, Walter was not going to bother anyone anymore.

About an hour later, two doctors slowly moved into the waiting room area to bring news about Joe's condition. The information we got consisted of a list of unknown possibilities for his injuries and recovery prospects. He was at least stable and not going to die, but long-term or how much damage Walter had done would need to wait for another day for more evaluation. Staying there would have been no benefit, and Jamie and I decided to go to the house and clean up the bloody mess of the prior evening.

We were not sure of the extent of what we would find, but by all accounts, there would be blood everywhere. We found nothing when we entered the house and passed into the kitchen. The entire house was spotless. There was no blood, nothing out of place, nothing as if the previous night's events had never occurred. We walked into the bedroom where the shooting took place and could see the police markers for where the bullet holes were around the room. Jamie and I were surprised Spring had made the bed, washed the clothes, folded them, and placed them neatly on the bed. Jamie and I stood and looked at each other; it felt strange that Spring would clean up the house only hours after a terrible event.

Leaving by the rear sliding door where Walter had made his entrance, we descended the stairs and walked along the path leading directly to the outdoor patio area. We found Spring smoking her cigarette there and pacing back and forth as if waiting for a newborn baby to arrive. I approached her and confronted the one person who could have prevented the entire event. "You caused this," I started. "You brought him here! You knew how he was! You knew he had issues with your father! You are one stupid bitch, you know that, don't you!" I concluded. Spring's defense echoes right back, "If I didn't go and get him, he threatened to kill the entire family; he threatened to kill me!" I stopped her mid-sentence, "Are you that stupid? Someone threatens to kill the family, and you go and get him and bring him to where the family is. Does that make any sense?"

Spring snaps back like a snake, "He had a gun, and I thought he was just going to blow off steam and leave ..." I stopped her again, "Did you try to call 911 or start to scream to alert your father? Did you do anything when he started up the path to the main house? The path only leads to the main house; where did you think he was going? Instead, you did nothing, you did nothing, and you may have gotten your father and mother killed. And you did get Walter killed!" Spring stepped back and loudly gasped, repeating slowly, "Walter's dead?" "Yes, and you were the cause; Walter is dead because of you; you're a stupid bitch." I ended. I turned and started to walk away when I had a final thought. Turning back, "If I were you, I would pack up and leave here. You are the cause and not welcome here anymore." Spring replied, "I'm not leaving here; I belong here. I am their daughter, and you are nothing, nothing. You hear me, nothing. Get out of here. I'm calling the police; get out!" I stopped for a moment to think about what Spring just said. "I am calling the police!" Looking directly at the person responsible for the attempted murder of her father, I slowly said, "Now, you are going to call the police. What happened last night when Walter was threatening them with a gun?" Spring said, "My phone was dead, and I could not call anybody." I stood momentarily, not believing what I had just heard from Spring. Spring was unaware that the neighbor across the street had spoken with me earlier that day and made a comment as to how Spring, after the shooting, stood in the driveway and talked on her telephone for two hours while the police conducted the homicide investigation inside the home. I watched her act defiant as she stood there broadcasting lies about the phone being dead. None of the events detailed by Spring matched what I had already learned from others at the scene or from the police. I now had more questions than answers as to why a person would allow someone with a gun to walk up the single path leading to where her parents were sleeping without a scream or some other warning.

Even more troubling was I could tell by Spring's reaction to the news that Walter was dead. There were still deep feelings. Whatever those feelings were, I could not imagine, but there were feelings. It must be true; people who suffer abuse fall in love with their abuser, as crazy as that may seem.

Joe Jr. and his wife Claudette arrived from New York late that afternoon. The family regrouped at the hospital shortly after they arrived and waited for whatever news would be forthcoming. After four P.M., the doctor revealed the extent of Joe's injuries and the most likely outcome. The doctor began with a description of the injuries, "Lucky, very lucky," the doctor began, "the bullet exited out and did not travel a path into the skull area. We can not save Joe's right eye, and I will attempt a reconstruction. Unfortunately, he will be blind in that eye. There are some small fragments in his nasal area, and we are going to leave them there; it is too risky to attempt removal, which could make things worse. He will be in pain for quite a while and need eye drops every few hours. Rest for the next few weeks will be a must. Other than that, he was fortunate." The doctor ended his update, turned, and left the room. We all just looked at each other and felt a sign of relief. Joe had escaped a bullet, literally, and this day in hell had ended, at least at the hospital. Now, it was time to deal with Spring.

We reconvened at my home and made plans for the following day. We all sat down at the island in my kitchen. Barbara sat in the middle, and everyone else surrounded her, almost forming a circle. I got to lead off the discussion, "I confronted Spring today, and what she told me was, at best, very disturbing. When Walter got to the guest house, he carried on for over fifteen minutes, destroying everything, and Spring did nothing. I asked her why she did not call 911 or scream, but she said nothing. And then she attempted to tell me her phone was dead, another lie. Spring admitted watching Walter walk up the path to the main house and taking no action besides lighting a cigarette. She answered that she thought Walter was going to blow off steam. I don't believe Spring knew what Walter intended to do, or at least I hope that was the case, but it leaves one problem. She did not at least try to stop him and give a warning to Joe and Barbara. I have a real problem with that, and I think she should not be allowed to stay." I ended my position there. We now looked toward Barbara to hear what she believed should happen. Barbara said in a low voice, "Well, maybe now that Walter is dead. She will be fine." I jumped back in, "No, she will not be fine. She almost got you and Joe killed because of her inaction, lies, and disregard. Barbara, this is not a time Spring can say, 'Oh, Walter's dead, and now I'm cured.'

She allowed the unthinkable to happen and has little or no remorse. If she had just tried to scream and alert you, I would be defending her, but she did not. She has lied for months about her and Walter, and now it's 'let bygones be bygones, or all is forgiven,' no way. Sorry, she is not going to be okay." Joe Jr. followed, "Ma, Spring has not been reasonable for a long time. I am sure it had to do with Walter, but there is something else. She is different and not the Spring we used to know. She needs help and the kind of help you can't give her. Maybe if she gets back on her own, she will realize that and get the help she needs. I think she needs to go also." With tears in her eyes, Barbara came to the reality that Spring could not stay.

At that meeting, we determined Spring would not voluntarily leave the guest house. We would need to file the paperwork for an order of protection against Spring with the local Court. Going this route would allow us time to sort out what happened and determine who was involved. The preparations for paperwork started the following day. I was assigned to write the details of events to support the court order, and Joe Jr., Claudette, and Barbara petitioned the Court for the order. The details of the partition were straightforward. Spring brought Walter back from Fort Myers; she knew he was armed, she knew he was making threats against the family, Spring was aware he was drunk that evening, and she did nothing to stop or intervene to prevent the attack. Finally, Barbara felt unsafe because of Spring's actions on that evening.

Joe Jr. filed the partition at ten thirty that morning, and the Judge granted it at four-thirty the same day. The order of protection issued demanded Spring vacate the guest house until a court date of seven days after serving the order.

Joe Jr. and Claudette met with the local sheriff's department around nine A.M. the next day. The sheriff accepted the service, and an officer was dispatched to execute the order of protection. The officer arrived at the guest house just before noon that same day. He knocked on the door, but there was no response. He struck the door again, followed by calling Spring's name, with the same result. The guest house appeared as if no one was home. The officer noticed a neighbor trimming his lawn as he was leaving. "Excuse me, sir, would you happen to know if Spring Thornton is home across the street," was the officer's question. The neighbor pointed to the car parked in the driveway before saying, "Well, that is her car; she should be there." "Thank you, that is what I suspected; I'll be back." The officer replied.

The officer returned within five minutes but parked the patrol car out of sight of the house this time. He quietly walked around the back of the guest house, and there stood Spring, smoking a cigarette and pacing back and forth. "You have been served," the officer shouted as Spring dashed for the safety of the guest house. The door slammed as the officer climbed the stairs. Speaking calmly, "Listen, if I need to call for backup, I will, but then

174

I will need to arrest you. Why not pack up some things, leave, and make this easy? Do you want to go to jail?" The door slowly opened, and Spring looked out and began her rant, "I'll go, I'll go, but I know who is behind all this, and I will not forget it. You let them know I will not forget all of this." Spring left with the officer's supervision and returned to Fort Myers to stay with her son.

Two weeks later, the court date for the order of protection was to go before the Court. Joe, Barbara, and I sat outside the courtroom door, waiting for the case to go before the Judge. Spring arrived with her sons in tow about half an hour after our arrival. She stopped directly in front of the three of us sitting on a bench and started with the same old crap holding and waving the court papers over her head, shouting. "Lies, lies, all of this is lies. I can't get a job in Florida, all because of these lies." I glanced up momentarily, thinking, "Spring has been here in Florida for almost three years and has not applied for a single job. I wondered how potential employers knew about these papers filed last week for the last three years?" Spring's body motions were quick and jerky as she continued. "I know who wrote all of these lies; he did." She pointed at me. With her arms flying over her head, she started speaking in a loud voice, "I am the victim here; I am the victim!" she wailed. It was then that an officer approached Spring. "Excuse me, are you the plaintiff or respondent, young lady?" Spring answered, "Respondent." The officer looked at Barbara, "Plaintiff or respondent?" Barbara replied, "Plaintiff." The officer turned back to Spring, "Young lady, I want you to go down to the other end of the hall and stay there. You come near these people again, and I will cuff you, do you understand?" Spring's face displayed total disgust at the officer's command. After all, she had not finished pointing out how much of a victim she was. She had not finished telling her parents it was all their fault, and none was hers. Spring did comply with the officer's command, moved to the end of the hall, and stayed there until the Judge called the case.

The case moved quickly, with Barbara dropping the charges supporting the order of protection if Spring would leave the guest house. Spring's words to the Judge, "I don't have anywhere to go," were brushed aside. Given two roads to travel, leave the guest house and go else-where or go to jail, Spring chose to leave. Finally, Spring and all the anger and grief she carried with her were gone.

To this day, I remember Spring's claim of her being the victim. As Spring's father sat there on the bench outside a courtroom suffering from a gunshot wound to the head, his right eye blown out and blind in that eye, her mother was still in shock from the event, and she, Spring, was the victim. I think Spring, in one sense, was right. Spring was a victim of herself and Walter but not the people who almost laid down their lives to help her. Spring, as bright as she was, could not identify the real cause of her problems. All of them were conceived and created from within.

One final note concerning Spring's and Walter's almost thirty-year relationship together. The word , but somewhere, through each of our deeds, within all of us lays the ability to create a limbo and condemn ourselves to life on earth in a mythical place we conceive. Here is where Spring and Walter spent their life together, and now Spring lives there without Walter to torment her, a true purgatory she created alone and where she currently resides.

Chapter Twenty-Two

Epliogue

Joe's and Barbara's lives have forever changed since the night of the hurricane. Joe is blind in the right eye, shot out by Walter, and struggles with other medical issues. The medical issues for Joe will continue for the rest of his life. Barbara has no memory of that night's events and is only aware of what others told her, which is probably good.

Since the night of the incident, the bedroom and kitchen areas have been repaired, the bullet-holed items removed, and the bedroom repainted, leaving only the ghost of tragic memories lying in wait. Joe and Barbara still awakened from sleep with the slightest out-of-place noise or movement. Their once peaceful home is no longer the safe refuge it was, and the family has installed security cameras.

My Brother Joe has forbidden the name of his daughter to be spoken by anyone in his home, and photos of Spring's family have been removed from the walls of Joe's and Barbara's home, leaving a void in their lives. Barbara tries to be more forgiving of her daughter, but Joe has brushed aside bed the voice of forgiveness. My observation is that if Barbara had been the person injured that evening, the forgiveness would not be as forthcoming.

Spring left the guest house following the day in court and moved back to Fort Myers, where her older son resides. Her claims of her, Spring, being the victim in what happened did not sit well with her father or, frankly, anyone else. Many people I have spoken with believe she may have been involved with what happened that night. I'll let the readers of this book decide for themselves, but I am giving her the benefit of the doubt and think she was stupid and scared. I believe Walter terrorized her to the point of total submission, and she did not know what to do. At least, I hope that is the case so she may find peace in her life, separated from her family.

Maybe, one day, she will look back at what led up to the incident and realize she was a significant cause of her father's near death, and then, too, maybe not.

CHAPTER TWENTY-THREE

Photo Gallery

Front driveway

Front view of house

Rear Guest House

Single Path Leading to Main House

Bedroom where attempted murder occurred

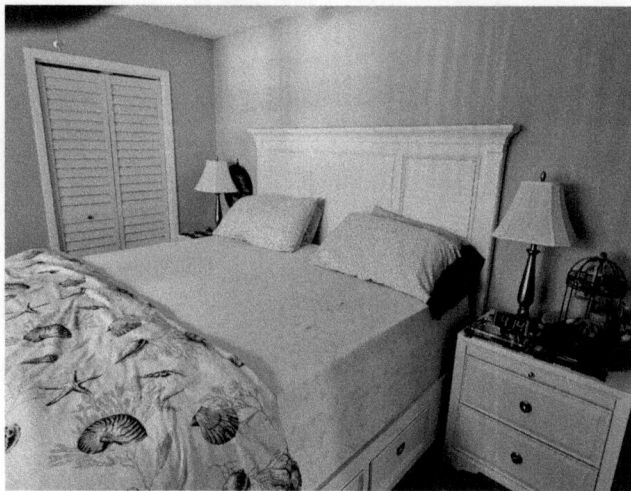

Bedroom where attempted murder occurred